Dutch Delight

Typical Dutch Food

Sylvia Pessireron
Jurjen Drenth & friends

N&L Publishing

colophon

Dutch Delight
Published by N&L Publishing **Produced by** Dutch Publishers **Concept** Allard de Rooi
Text Sylvia Pessireron **Editor** Martijn de Rooi **Photography** Jurjen Drenth & friends*
Design Maarten van der Kroft **Studio photography** Arthur van der Laan, OXBird.nl
Production and photo editing Jeff Zimberlin, Arend-Jan de Vos, Wendy Meijerink
Translation Linda Cook, Paul Rueckert, Nellie Werner and Tekom Vertalers, Hoofd-
dorp (info@tekom.nl) **Printing** Scholma Druk, Bedum (www.scholma.nl) **Thanks to**
Hilde Verweij, Hetty van Oijen and Aurora Lum Chou for styling and cooking, and to
Dennis Bosch for additional design

ISBN 90-8541-011-8
First printing June 2005

Trade distribution Nilsson & Lamm BV, P.O. Box 195, 1380 AD Weesp,
the Netherlands. Telephone: 0294 494 949. E-mail: info@nilsson-lamm.nl.

Dutch Publishers and **Dutch Image** are registered trade names of **The Ad Agency**,
P.O. Box 340, 2400 AH Alphen aan den Rijn, the Netherlands. Telephone: 0172 449 333.
Fax: 0172 495 846. Internet: www.theadagency.nl. E-mail: info@theadagency.nl.

* **Friends are** Allard de Rooi, Arend-Jan de Vos, Arthur van der Laan, Femke Diets,
Hein Hage, Hetty van Oijen, Maarten van der Kroft, Martijn de Rooi, Wendy Meijerink
and Wilbert Collet.

The photos in this book are provided by Dutch Image.
t: 0172 449 330 i: **www.dutchimage.nl** e: info@dutchimage.nl

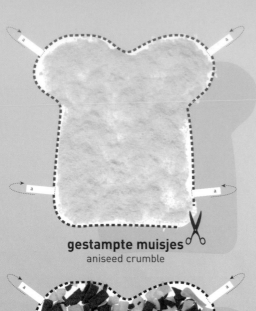

gestampte muisjes
aniseed crumble

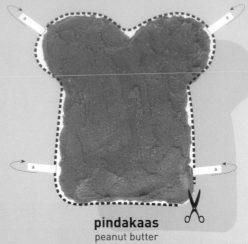

pindakaas
peanut butter

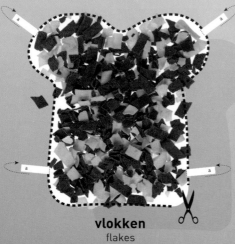

vlokken
flakes

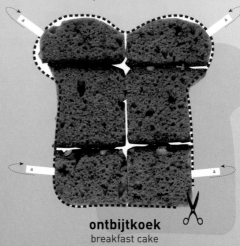

ontbijtkoek
breakfast cake

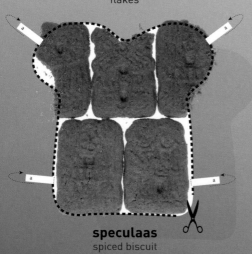

speculaas
spiced biscuit

hagelslag
hundreds and thousands

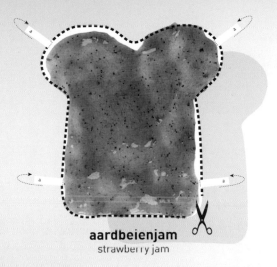

aardbeienjam
strawberry jam

place topping
of your
choice here

boterham
sandwich

bread & toppings

06→ bread   **10→** sandwich fillings

Dutch people eat far more bread than other Europeans. About sixty kilograms of bread are consumed per person per year in the Low Countries. And no other country boasts as many ways to dress up a sandwich.

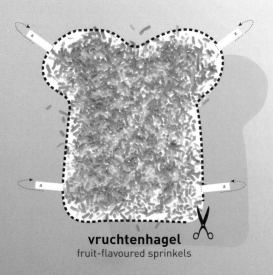

vruchtenhagel
fruit-flavoured sprinkels

appelstroop
apple spread

01

many-sided everyday fare

THE DUTCH ARE TRUE BREAD-EATERS. THEY CONSUME TWO BREAD-BASED MEALS A DAY: BREAKFAST AND LUNCH. THEREFORE, IN THE LOW COUNTRIES 'PUTTING BREAD ON THE TABLE' IS MORE THAN JUST A FIGURE OF SPEECH. AND NO OTHER COUNTRY BOASTS SO MANY VARIETIES OF BREAD.

Bread is important to Dutch people. Not just as a side dish or as a simple accompaniment to a meal, but as the meal itself. 'Our daily bread' is served twice a day, to the disappointment of many a foreign guest. But those who take pains to discover the great variety of Dutch bread sorts will understand why the Dutch just don't seem to get enough of it.

Black and white

Agriculture has determined the face of the Dutch landscape for generations. Grains such as wheat, rye, oats, buckwheat and barley were always readily available, which meant that bread could be baked anywhere.

In times past, the consumption of bread was roughly split between the 'white bread eaters' in the west of the country and the 'black bread eaters' in the east and south. Wheat was more expensive than rye, so wealthier families were more likely to eat white bread made from wheat, while poorer people had to get by with black bread made from rye.

Only on Sundays and holidays was white bread served in less well-to-do families, and then only as a topping on a slice of black bread. 'Because,' grumbled the common man, 'you need to eat black bread to be able to work'. In those days, there was not yet a consensus on the greater nutritional value of black bread versus white.

Spiced and incised

After the Second World War, the Netherlands was awash with cheap American wheat, which meant that wheat bread was available to everyone. Bakeries shot up like mushrooms and sold their bread in shops or from carts that were pushed through the streets. A standard loaf of Dutch bread was made from wheat flour, water, a pinch of salt and yeast. This simple recipe was toyed with endlessly over the years to achieve even tastier results.

Milk is now sometimes used instead of water, as is buttermilk, which makes the bread softer and gives it a slightly sour taste. Even beer is used in some recipes. The addition of butter, cooking fat or oil gives bread a softer structure that is typical of deluxe rolls, croissants or a *duivekater*, a special kind of bread baked in certain parts of the country to help ring in the New Year.

Light, individual sponge cakes and crispy baked rolls are made from bread dough with lots of eggs whisked in. Sugar, sultanas and currants are key ingredients in sweet loaves such as cinnamon bread and currant bread, and a pungent or spicy flavour can be obtained by adding herbs and spices to the dough. Savoury ingredients such as cheese, meat or fish can almost turn a simple bread roll into a complete meal. Sprinkling bread with oat flakes, sesame seeds or poppy seeds makes the bread attractive and

The aroma of freshly baked bread is more seductive than the scent of the partner to whom one has just made love, a study shows.

03 Baker with baker's cart in Gorinchem in 1980, a scene which has become rare in the present-day Netherlands **04** Old-fashioned sign on the bakery Out, Ouderkerk aan de Amstel

02

GY SIET MY AEN, EN
KUNT NIETS HOOREN
TREE MAER IN HUYS
WY KOMEN VOREN

03

04

enhances the taste in a subtle way. The structure and taste of bread can also be enlivened with oats, sunflower seeds, soybeans or buckwheat. These additions change the bread's nutritional value, too. And, finally, the dough can be braided, it can be round or egg-shaped, incised, baked as mini-loaves or rolls, baked in tins the shape of animals or flowers, or in standard, rectangular baking tins. All these variations result in an almost infinite range of bread sorts in the Netherlands.

TRY ME →

French toast (Wentelteefjes)

A tasty way to eat stale bread.

Ingredients (serves 2-4)

4 slices (stale) bread
2 eggs
1 dl milk
2 tsp cinnamon
butter
caster sugar

Preparation

Whisk egg, milk, and cinnamon together in a mixing bowl. Dip a slice of bread into the mixture, letting it soak in. Heat a dollop of butter in a frying pan. Remove the bread from the egg and milk mixture and fry for three to five minutes on a medium/high heat until brown on both sides. Serve with caster sugar and cinnamon.

Floury verse

In order to keep putting bread on the table, both literally and figuratively, many bakers in the 1950s tried their hand at a bit of doggerel verse. They hung little rhymes and poems outside their shops in the hope of attracting more customers.

A baker called Terbeek, from the town of Almelo, came up with the slogan 'Six days a week, get your bread from Terbeek'. To which a rival baker called Vialach added, 'And on the seventh day in Almelo, Vialach's is the place to go'. Terbeek was a good sport and left this second line of verse intact for years.

But nothing works quite as well as the aroma of freshly baked bread when it comes to attracting customers. In one study into the appeal of different smells, the aroma of freshly baked bread came in at first place, followed by the smell of newly mown grass and fresh coffee. The scent of the partner to whom one has just made love finished way behind.

Wedding and birthday bread

Variations on the theme of bread play a role in a number of festive occasions. The birth of a child is celebrated with Dutch rusks sprinkled with aniseed comfits (called muisjes, 'mice'), the colour of the sugary, aniseed sprinkles denoting the sex of the child – blue for a boy, pink for a girl.

In Twente, in the east of the country, great ceremony is employed when presenting midwives with a krentenwegge, a ridiculously long white loaf filled with currants. The loaf is laid on a ladder – the only thing long enough to hold it, and two men carry the ladder into the house on their shoulders, to the surprise of the new mother and the satisfaction of the midwife.

In some parts of the country, weddings provide an opportunity for some very special baking. One particular loaf, the wikkelkindje, or wrapped-up baby, is a subtle hint to the bride to concentrate on the business of producing babies. ∎

07 The popular Geitebreier (old duffer) roll of the Kleywegs Stadskoffiehuis in Delft **09** Scene from a famous commercial for King Corn, American white bread which was very popular in the 1970s **10** Baking bread according to traditional methods in the Bakery Museum in Luyckgestel **13** Important Dutch ritual: having breakfast with the family **15** Leiden baker Arend Oostwaert and his wife Catharina Keyzerswaert, painted circa 1638 by Jan Steen **17** Bakery Bert van Haren in Den Bosch, founded in 1883 in an 15th-century building

SANDWICH FILLINGS

master decorators

THE ART OF DECORATING BREAD HAS REACHED ITS PERFECTION IN THE NETHER-
LANDS. FOREIGNERS ARE STUPEFIED BY THE INCREDIBLE VARIATION OF DUTCH
TOPPINGS, AND ESPECIALLY BY THE INNUMERABLE FORMS OF CANDY THE DUTCH
SPREAD AND SPRINKLE ON THEIR BREAD.

02 Schoolkids having lunch
03 Different kinds of sprinkles

When sprinkled thickly, chocolate sprinkles can cover a slice of bread with as much chocolatey goodness as half a bar of the real thing.

Connoisseurs regard the Dutch as master decorators – *sandwich* decorators, that is. First, they carefully spread a generous layer of butter or margarine on their sandwich before going on to choose a savoury or sweet filling. Peanut butter, jam, chocolate spread or sprinkles, sugary aniseed crumble, fruit-flavoured sprinkles, hazelnut or apple spread, cheese, liver sausage, ham or other luncheon meats are all part of their impressive arsenal. If they're feeling adventurous they might top their cheese sandwich with slices of banana or spread some jam or fiery red pepper paste on their cheese. A sandwich topped with peanut butter *and* chocolate sprinkles is doubly sweet and a real treat for many people.

Sound fillings

Dutch children love to choose fillings for their sandwiches and one of the first things they learn is to eat a savoury sandwich first and a sweet sandwich second. Responsible parents know that eating only sweet toppings will make children overly plump, and cause them to miss out on the healthy nutrition offered by fibre-rich breads topped with luncheon meats or cheese.

Most Dutch children really learn to enjoy eating bread when it is spread with a generous layer of peanut butter, meat paste or liver pâté. And since one's first love is remembered one's whole life long, these simple fillings remain popular long into adulthood.

Develish topping

These days, topping bread with all kinds of goodies is taken for granted. But it wasn't so long ago that sandwich fillings were reserved for special occasions. Bread with honey or sugar was reserved for a special treat for Sunday tea or birthday parties. And instead of butter, which was something of a luxury, lard was used to which a dollop of treacle had been added. Cheese was only used as a sandwich filling in traditional dairy regions such as the provinces of Friesland and North and South Holland. And when eating cheese, butter was never used. In the eyes of the God-fearing common man cheese and butter was a wasteful – and dangerous – extravagance, for 'dairy upon dairy, that makes the Devil merry'.

Chocolate sprinkles

Chocolate is a common filling for sandwiches in the Netherlands. Not as a whole bar, but subtly packed as sprinkles or confetti (*hagelslag*, which literally means 'hail'). When sprinkled thickly, chocolate sprinkles can cover a slice of bread with as much chocolatey goodness as half a bar of the real thing. One tall tale about the origins of chocolate *hagelslag* goes as follows. The inventor of chocolate sprinkles was a Norwegian named Rolle Hagl, who was a

trader in sealskins. He awoke one morning to find his cupboards empty of anything to spread on his morning bread. He hated eating bread with just butter, and since the nearest shop was a week's walk away, he cudgelled a bar of chocolate into small pieces, which he then sprinkled onto his bread. His example met with an enthusiastic response, so he patented it and later traded his patent to the Dutchman Henk Venz for a bottle of gin.

Unfortunately there is not a grain of truth in the story, for the Venz family never existed. Venz is however the name of the Netherlands' biggest producer of chocolate sprinkles, but the name is an acronym derived from the words De *Vries en Z*onen (De Vries and Sons). According to the Venz factory, it was Gerard, son of the firm's founder, who first came up with the idea for chocolate sprinkles. In 1936 he developed a machine to turn his dream of shiny chocolate sprinkles into reality.

Today, *hagelslag* is available in bitter chocolate, milk chocolate and bitter chocolate with vanilla. Chocolate, or rather cocoa, is not just the main ingredient in chocolate sprinkles, but also in milk chocolate flakes and chocolate spread.

Peanut butter: good for you!

No one else in the world eats more peanut butter than the Dutch and the Americans. Whether peanut butter is healthy for you or not has long been a matter of debate. Recent studies indicate that peanut butter aficionados may indulge themselves to their heart's content. Eating two dessertspoons of peanut butter a day will provide the peanut butter lover with all the vitamins and minerals the peanut has to offer. Furthermore, it seems that the fats in peanut butter can aid in lowering levels of cholesterol.

Sweet sandwich fillings have really only featured regularly on Dutch dining tables since the 1950s. But the habit of eating bread with meat has been around for centuries. The top ten of Dutch meats for sandwiches starts with liver sausage, then *snijworst*, shoulder of ham, gammon and *boterhamworst*. (*Snijworst* and *boterhamworst* are both types of luncheon meat).

Apart from those, there are some tasty regional specialities. A visit to the city of Utrecht is not complete without sampling a *broodje Vocking*, or Vocking sandwich. The recipe for this classic Utrecht liver sausage has remained a closely guarded secret of the Vocking family for more than a century. ∎

04 The tight bond between the Dutch and their daily bread
05 Famous all over the country: sandwich bar Broodje van Coot in Utrecht **06** Flipje, the famous mascot of jam producer De Betuwe, present-day Hero

Fruity Flipje

Alongside chocolate and peanut butter, jam is also popular in Dutch sandwiches. The fruit used in Dutch jams comes from the Betuwe region of the Netherlands and it was here that the first jam factory was founded. Under the name *Betuwsche Jam*, the firm of De Betuwe (nowadays known as Hero) brought the first varieties of jam on to the market. As more jam factories were set up in the region, the firm was taken to court and forced to change its brand name.

In a decisive move, the management called for the design of a new mascot. The Amsterdam-based advertising agency responsible for design of the Piet Pelle figure for the Gazelle bicycle factory and the mascot for the Droste chocolate factory was approached for a new mascot, and in 1934 Flipje was born. With a body of raspberries and berry-shaped limbs to match, Flipje, with his white chef's hat, was the unchallenged icon of jam-loving Dutch folk right up to the late 1970s.

06

dairy

01

Dairy produce is, alongside clogs, tulips and windmills, one of the first things that foreigners associate with Holland. Dairy products from the Low Countries enjoy an unbeatable reputation worldwide and no country exports more cheese, butter or powdered milk than the country of 'cheese-heads'.

01

milk mania

THE NETHERLANDS IS THE COUNTRY OF MILK AND HONEY-SWEET MILK-BASED PRODUCTS. SOME TWO MILLION DUTCH COWS EACH PRODUCE AN AVERAGE OF 35 LITRES OF MILK A DAY. THIS MAKES THE DUTCH DAIRY COW AN UNDISPUTED WORLD CHAMPION, AND THE DUTCH THE GREATEST MILK CONSUMER IN THE WORLD.

02

The Dutch consume an average of 140 litres of dairy produce each year – more than any other nation in the world. Their fridges will always contain a selection of full-fat milk, skimmed milk, milk with added calcium, fruit-flavoured milk, buttermilk and milk straight from the farm. And next to these will be several varieties of cheese (SEE PAGE 20), butter, margarine, cartons of yoghurt, *vla* (cold, flavoured custard), or one of a myriad of flavoured, milk-based desserts of which the Dutch are so fond (SEE PAGE 62 AND 65).

School milk

This high rate of consumption is not only attributable to the huge supply of milk and milk products in the Netherlands, but is also the result of extensive promotional campaigns. The Dutch government was the first to initiate such a campaign.
In the early 1930s there was wide concern at the growth rate of city children, which lagged behind that of their counterparts in the country. Not only were city kids smaller, they also fell ill more frequently. At the same time, the country was dealing with an enormous milk surplus, and many dairies and farming communities were facing deep crisis. School milk turned out to be the answer. In 1937, the Central Committee for School Milk was set up to organise the provision of subsidised milk to all primary schools. For decades, the milk float, piled high with crates of milk bottles, was a common sight at school gates throughout the country. The crates were distributed among schoolrooms early in the morning; in winter they were placed next to

The Dutch consume an average of 140 litres of dairy produce each year – more than any other nation in the world.

the radiators for fear that cold milk would upset for children's delicate stomachs. Around mid-morning, each pupil received a quarter of a litre of full-fat milk, easily recognisable by the dollop of cream floating on top.

01 The mechanical process of milking **03** Campina school milk in the varieties fat, low-fat, strawberry and chocolate

03

The white engine

Milk consumption was further stimulated by intensive advertising campaigns. One of them depicted a cartoon character, Joris Driepinter (Joris Three-pinter), who informed the nation that each child needed at least three glasses of milk a day to remain healthy and be able to concentrate well. Joris was succeeded by a series of successful slogans, such as: 'Milk – it does a body good', 'Milk – everyone needs it', and 'Milk – the white engine', slogans that remain etched forever in the collective Dutch memory.

These campaigns seemed to pay off. Due partly to the increased consumption of dairy products, the Dutch started to shoot up like vines. These days, each generation is, on average, 4.5 cm taller than the previous one and the Dutch have risen to become the tallest nation in the world. And there are no signs that they will fall short of this record – the growth spurt continues. School milk is no longer distributed to all primary schools, and the dairy industry now targets its advertising at other demographic groups – the elderly for example. Many older people believe they don't need to consume as much dairy produce as they used to. But now that the elderly live longer and are more active than in previous generations, they actually need more of the nutrients that milk provides.

Go suck a yoghurt

However, the dairy industry is still doing its best to keep the younger generation interested in its products. Supermarket shelves are crammed with new-look packaging and appetising flavours, and more are being introduced all the time.

The latest craze is 'yoghurt-in-a-bag', with a kind of nipple attachment through which you suck up the yoghurt, available in cherry, peach and pine nut flavours. It may not sound very attractive but it has certainly caught on. Thousands of teenagers are currently addicted to slurping up the yoghurt drink; they apparently think it looks cool. For those who consider it too childish, 'drink yoghurt' can also be bought in cartons – in a range of flavours including peach, strawberry, raspberry and banana.

04

05

The porridge revolution

Many of the older generation in The Netherlands think back nostalgically to their youth, long before the days of suck-up yoghurt, or even computers. For them, breakfast meant a wholesome bowl of porridge that was made by cooking finely ground cereal with milk for hours on end. Left to thicken overnight, it was heated up for breakfast the next morning, diluted with more milk.

After the Second World War, the introduction of pre-cooked oats and wheat flakes triggered a revolution in porridge preparation. Now, milk only needed warming before being poured over the rolled oats or *Brinta* (wheat flakes). Enthusiastic articles in popular magazines were partly responsible for the transformation of porridge from its status as a simple, 'worker's breakfast' to a healthy start to the day from which no child could escape.

Unfortunately, modern cooking techniques were unable to solve the problem of the skins that form on porridge as it cools, and many people retain traumatic memories of their childhood as a result. It did, however, help them grow to become the strapping Dutch adults they are today. ■

TRY ME ➡

Traditional Dutch chocolate milk

Milk mixed with chocolate will turn even the greatest milk hater into a milk addict.

Ingredients (serves 4)

8 dl milk	2 egg yolks
160 g dark chocolate	3 tbsp sugar

Preparation

Grate the chocolate finely. In a saucepan, bring the milk to the boil and add the grated chocolate. Stir until the chocolate has melted. Bring to the boil once again and remove from the heat. Whisk egg yolks and sugar together in a large bowl until they start to froth. Add the milk and chocolate mixture and whisk thoroughly. Serve in glasses.

08 'Yoghurt-in-a-bag'

Skal 1865

01

CHEESE

say cheese

THE NETHERLANDS IS THE WORLD'S NUMBER ONE CHEESE PRODUCER. SHOPS ARE PILED HIGH WITH VARIETIES RANGING FROM THE FAMOUS *GOUDA* AND *EDAM* TO LESSER-KNOWN SORTS SUCH AS FRISIAN CLOVE CHEESE. IT'S HARDLY SURPRISING THEN THAT THE DUTCH HAVE BEEN NICKNAMED 'CHEESE-HEADS'.

Deutsches Bier und echter Käse aus Holland!

01 Traditional way of transporting cheese at the famous cheese market in Gouda **02** German advertisement featuring Frau Antje: 'German beer and real Dutch cheese go together very well' **04** Relief at the old weighhouse for cheese, built in 1668, in Gouda

'Cheese-head' is actually a derogatory term for a Dutch person that originates in Belgium, yet the nickname might just as well be interpreted as a hard-won compliment. The Dutch tradition of cheese making is as rich as it is long; in fact it can be traced all the way back to ancient history. Archaeologists have unearthed primitive pottery that suggests that the Lowlands had already mastered the art of cheese making in prehistoric times. And none other than Julius Caesar himself gave a description of the very same skill in the 1st century BC.

Maid in Holland

The Dutch first started shipping their cheeses overseas towards the end of the Middle Ages. As well as being eaten, the imported cheese was also used as a unit of currency, for buying rights of passage on a river, for example. By the time the Hollanders had achieved world trade domination at the height of the Dutch Golden Age (1585 to 1670) their homeland had acquired the irrefutable reputation as the one and only 'cheese country'.

Around 1960 that status was reinforced by a blonde milkmaid in national costume promoting Dutch cheese all over Germany. Frau Antje was her name, and her huge success led to countless other Dutch milkmaids spreading the word to other parts of the world.

Gouda and Edam

Today the Netherlands leads the world in cheese export. Close to 700 million kilos of cheese are produced here each year, with roughly three-quarters destined for overseas consumption. One of the best-known Dutch cheeses is manufactured in the town of Gouda. The large, bright yellow 'wagon wheels' weigh in at some twelve kilos each. Gouda cheese comes in several varieties; the longer the cheese has been left to mature, the stronger its flavour. Equally famous, though produced on a smaller scale, are the distinctive round cheeses made in Edam. These are formed in a spherical mould called a 'cheese-head' (which brings us back to those name-calling Belgians). Edam cheeses produced for export are conserved in an eye-catching waxy coating of red paraffin. Like Gouda cheese, *Edam* is available in many different flavours, from mild to strong.

Both towns, Gouda and Edam, hold folkloric cheese markets during the summer months that give a good impression of Holland's cheese trading past. The town of Alkmaar also puts on a cheese market that is well worth a visit. There you can see traditional cheese carriers at work, transporting cheeses up and down the market from springtime through to autumn. This practice dates back centuries; in fact

The nickname 'cheese-head' is actually a Belgian derogatory term for a Dutch person.

07 Husband and wife running a cheese farm in Haastrecht **08** Cheese carriers in action at the famous cheese market in Alkmaar **10** Cutting cheese at the ecological cheese farm Vicarienerf in Leusden **11** Map of the Mecca of cheese, the Netherlands, designed by Dutch Publishers

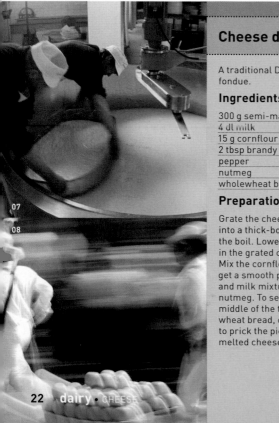

07

08

TRY ME →

Cheese dip

A traditional Dutch variation on cheese fondue.

Ingredients (serves 4)

300 g semi-mature Gouda cheese
4 dl milk
15 g cornflour
2 tbsp brandy
pepper
nutmeg
wholewheat bread cut into small squares

Preparation

Grate the cheese roughly. Pour the milk into a thick-bottomed saucepan and bring to the boil. Lower the flame and gradually stir in the grated cheese until it has all melted. Mix the cornflour with the brandy until you get a smooth paste, then add to the cheese and milk mixture. Season with pepper and nutmeg. To serve, place the saucepan in the middle of the table with a plate of whole-wheat bread, cut into squares. Use a fork to prick the pieces of bread and dip into the melted cheese mixture.

09

10

the cheese carriers had organised themselves into a guild as far back as 1619.

Sweet, spicy and smoked

Apart from selling Edam and Gouda, a typical Dutch cheese counter will display a host of other varieties to challenge the taste buds. One favourite is the 'holey' *Maasdammer*, with its distinctive sweet, nutty taste. Another popular cheese is *Leidse*, or cumin cheese, highly seasoned with cumin seeds. Cumin is also one of the ingredients in the strong Frisian clove cheese, made with skimmed milk and spiced with cumin seeds and cloves.

The Dutch are very inventive when it comes to adding herbs and spices; they even have a nettle-flavoured cheese. Yet even within the range of the 'regular' cheeses, there is an almost infinite variety. Rich cream cheese, different cheese spreads, smoked cheeses, goat's cheeses and sheep's cheeses in many sorts and flavours – these are just a handful from a seemingly endless selection of cheese guaranteed to make any cheese-lover's mouth water.

Sliced up nice

The Dutch are not just known for their cheese, but also for the utensil they use to slice it so thinly and evenly. The Dutch cheese slicer is, for some, the ultimate symbol of Dutch thriftiness.

Yet the famous cheese slicer is not a Dutch invention. The credit goes to a carpenter from the Norwegian town of Lillehammer, who came up with the idea back in 1925. However, the slicer was quickly adopted by a nation for whom frugality is traditionally a virtue. The cheese slicer has even made its mark on Dutch politics, where the equal distribution of economic measures over a number of ministries, organisations or departments is called the 'cheese slicer method'. ■

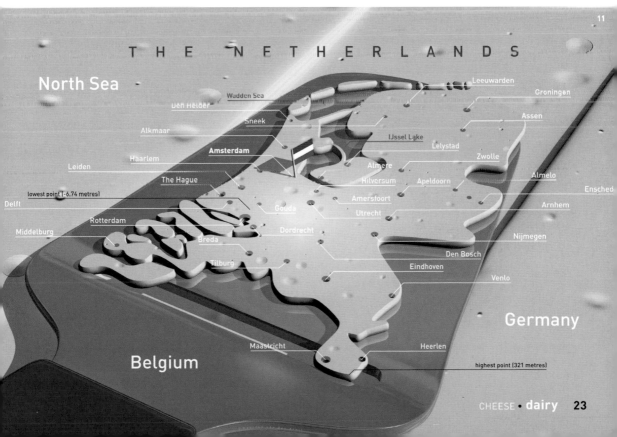

THE NETHERLANDS

North Sea

Wadden Sea

Leeuwarden

Groningen

Den Helder

Assen

Sneek

Alkmaar

IJssel Lake

Lelystad

Zwolle

Amsterdam

Almere

Almelo

Haarlem

Enschede

Leiden

Hilversum

Apeldoorn

The Hague

lowest point (-6.74 metres)

Amersfoort

Arnhem

Delft

Gouda

Utrecht

Rotterdam

Dordrecht

Nijmegen

Middelburg

Breda

Den Bosch

Tilburg

Eindhoven

Venlo

Germany

Maastricht

Heerlen

Belgium

highest point (321 metres)

The Dutch only consider their most popular soup – *snert*, thick pea soup –
a success if they can stand up a spoon in it. Foreign visitors often question
whether, with such a consistency, it can still be called 'soup'. Indeed, they
might well use the other meaning of *snert* to describe it: 'worthless'.

02

healthy snack or complete meal

ONCE THE DUTCH MAINLY ATE HEAVY SOUPS, CONSIDERED AS COMPLETE MEALS. TODAY SOUP IS EATEN AS A MULTIFUNCTIONAL, OFTEN 'TRENDY' STARTER, A NUTRITIOUS PICK-ME-UP AND – HOW TIMES HAVE CHANGED – A POPULAR FOOD FOR THOSE TRYING TO LOSE WEIGHT. NONETHELESS, THE THICK SOUPS ARE STILL VERY POPULAR.

TRY ME →

Pea soup

A true Dutch Delight.

Ingredients (serves 8)

250 g dried green peas	1 smoked sausage
250 g dried split peas	a sprinkling of thyme
1 onion	2 bay leaves
1 large carrot	2 leeks
a pinch of salt	1 celeriac root
a pinch of freshly ground	3 potatoes
black pepper	1 bunch of parsley
one 400 g pork cutlet	1 head of celery
250 g smoked bacon	rye bread
rashers	

Preparation

Wash the green peas and soak them overnight (split peas do not need soaking). Peel and chop the onion and peel and dice the carrot. Bring a large pan of water to the boil and add the peas, onion, carrot, salt, pepper, pork cutlet, thyme and bay leaves. Simmer for two hours. Wash and slice the leeks. Peel and dice the celeriac root and the potatoes. Add vegetables to the soup and simmer for 45 minutes. Add the sausage and let it steep for a further fifteen minutes making sure the soup doesn't boil. Take out the pork cutlet, sausage and bay leaves. Slice the cutlet and the sausage and put the pieces back in the soup. Flavour the soup with the washed and chopped celery and parsley; add salt and pepper to taste. Let the soup stand overnight. Before serving, warm it on a low heat and stir regularly to prevent it burning. Dutch pea soup is traditionally served with rashers of smoked bacon on rye bread.

03

The history of Dutch soup is quite straightforward. The heavier soups, like pea soup, which were usually eaten as complete meals, date back to the Middle Ages when both food and fuel were hard to come by and most people didn't have two cents to rub together.

Until 1940, those living in the country knew of no other first course than soup. It was considered something of a luxury and tended to be reserved for Sundays or for visitors. It had to be a thin, clear soup. The thicker pea soups or bean soups were for labourers on weekdays. Clear soups had a certain status, but to raise them above the level of flavoured water, a handful of rice or vermicelli was often thrown in.

Saturday is soup day

Canned soup first made its appearance in the Netherlands in 1957. It was Unox, better known for its sausages, who were prepared to gamble on the success of soup-in-a-tin. In the beginning, they could only turn out twelve large pans of soup a day, so production was limited to a small amount of tomato soup.

However, as the Dutch realised how convenient soup in a tin actually was, the assortment grew to include vegetable, pea and oxtail soup. Indeed, Unox was so eager to stimulate consumption that it gave away 2.9 million cans of soup in 1961. The promotion was a great success. The Dutch claimed Saturday as traditional 'soup' day and the name Unox was forever linked with soup in the minds of the Dutch.

Daily 'soup fix'

These days, soup makes an excellent appetiser and can usually be made to blend perfectly with the courses that follow. Shops and supermarkets are full of different varieties, from the exotic to instant soups, which are hugely popular in the Netherlands, especially amongst the working population. Indeed, it is widely felt that today's office workers need their daily 'soup fix'. The majority can choose

04

from different soup flavours in office drink dispensers throughout the country. If it was left to soup marketers, the Dutch would eat soup every day.

The spoon test

Of all the traditional Dutch soups, pea soup is by far the most well known and is a winter speciality, served throughout the season as a full, and fulfilling, meal in itself. Pea soup which is made a day in advance is called snert. As the peas cool, the soup thickens to such an extent that purists argue that it can no longer be called 'soup'. One should, they insist, be able to pour or drink soup; snert can only be eaten with a spoon.

The Dutch however, would apply the other meaning of the word snert – 'worthless' – to such an argument. They test whether their soup has reached the right consistency by standing a spoon in it. If the spoon stands up straight, it's perfect.

Queen's soup

Of course, there are more soups in the Dutch kitchen than pea soup. The healthiest is probably what's known as 'farmer's vegetable' soup. Full of fresh vegetables and herbs, it's also low in calories, which makes it popular with slimmers.

If you like a heartier soup, there's brown bean soup, and among the lighter soups clear chicken consommé is a favourite. Chicken soup made with flour and cream has earned the regal title 'queen's soup'. And then there's linke soep. Not really applicable to soup at all, and especially not to snert, it means 'risky business'. ■

04 Unox pea soup-in-a-tin

Chicken soup made with flour and cream has earned the regal title 'queen's soup'.

Potatoes and vegetables
are prime components
of the Dutch hot meal.
Vegetable-lovers as
they are, the Dutch also
generally have a salad on
the table. Fresh fruit, on
the other hand, isn't very
popular.

potatoes, vegetables & fruit

cherished and versatile tuber

MANY PEOPLE FIND IT HARD TO BELIEVE, BUT THE COMMON SPUD ALMOST ALWAYS PLAYS A LEADING ROLE IN THE DUTCH MAIN MEAL OF THE DAY. HOWEVER, THE HUMBLE STATUS OF THIS LOWLY TUBER BELIES ITS TRUE NATURE. UNDER THE SKIN IS AN EXTREMELY VERSATILE VEGETABLE.

POTATOES

01

'What would a Dutch meal be like without potatoes?' 'Less bland and more imaginative', might be the answer from many a potato hater. But such a cliché is an insult to this low profile, high-yield crop. For most Dutch people, a hot meal without potatoes is like a bicycle without pedals or a windmill without vanes. Whether boiled, fried or deep-fried, potatoes are an indispensable part of Dutch cuisine.

Vast potential

The potato first appeared in the Netherlands around 1600. Initially, potatoes were cultivated sporadically and only the leaves were eaten. They nearly disappeared from the culinary landscape when they caused a series of deaths; the potato is a close relative of the poisonous deadly nightshade. It was only when people became more knowledgeable about the potato itself, and realised that it could be eaten, that cultivation began on a large scale.

It wasn't long before the potato's vast potential came to light: it flourished in all kinds of soil, yielded enormous harvests, and the flavour improved rapidly as new cultivation techniques emerged. And the humble potato even saved lives when famine threatened in the mid-18th century as the result of a ruined grain harvest and cattle plague epidemics. The typically Dutch dish *stamppot*, a kind of hotchpotch or bubble

01 A family in Nuenen during dinner. The tableau resembles the famous painting *The Potato Eaters*, which Vincent van Gogh painted in the same village

and squeak (SEE PAGE 34) in which the potato is the key ingredient, originates from this period.

Rise to stardom

The potato has come a long way from its early beginnings as a measly root. It went on to become an indispensable ingredient in the kitchens of Europe, a source of inspiration for the world-famous painter Vincent van Gogh, and the single most important ingredient in McDonald's French fries.

In the Netherlands, potatoes are nearly always accompanied by meat and vegetables. The consumer can choose between an astounding 250 potato varieties that all differ in colour, taste, shape and method of preparation. Each variety is cultivated for a specific purpose: some for cooking and others for processing into crisps or frozen chips.

The real potato enthusiast knows that there are three basic potato types: waxy, crumbly and extra crumbly. Waxy potatoes retain their shape during boiling while crumbly potatoes tend to break apart somewhat. Extra crumbly potatoes, also known as mushy potatoes, disintegrate completely. The first two types are suitable for most dishes, while the last is generally reserved for soups, soufflés and purée.

The consumer can choose between an astounding 250 potato varieties that all differ in colour, taste, shape and method of preparation.

04
05
06

Little Miss Potato

By far the most well-known and most popular variety of potato in the Netherlands is the *bintje*, created by Frisian schoolmaster De Vries, who together with his pupils experimented with the cultivation of new varieties of potatoes. Every new potato they came up with was named after one of the schoolchildren.

One of his favourite pupils was a sturdy but charming Frisian girl, Bintje Jansma. The best potato variety they produced was therefore given her name: *bintje*. It would be pure speculation to try and establish just what qualities the schoolmaster thought the one *bintje* had in common with the other Bintje, but the fact is that the *bintje* is no ordinary potato. It is a spud of Olympian proportion: large, round, firm, with attractive colouring and a pleasant flavour. No other variety of potato in the world produces such large harvests, can be cultivated in so many different climates and soil types and has so many different uses. And all this thanks to schoolmaster De Vries and Bintje.

It's a riot

However, success also has its downside. Just how important the potato had become to the average Dutch citizen became obvious during the bloody potato riots of 1917. There was a tremendous food shortage throughout Europe during the years of the Great War. Potatoes especially were scarce. Yet the export of potatoes from the Netherlands was allowed to continue, to the great dismay of the populace.

Anger over the exports came to a head in the summer of 1917 when groups of Amsterdam housewives attempted to commandeer a consignment of potatoes. The police intervened and the situation escalated within a matter of days. By way of compromise, the unruly women were offered access to the great stores of rice, but these were resolutely rejected: 'If I serve that up for my husband I'll never hear the end of it!' And so, as an interesting footnote to this story, the potato won its first glorious victory over that other popular staple.

But that was neither here nor there to the housewives of 1917. Hunger and desperation drove the women to storm trains and boats for their supplies of potatoes and cauliflower. The Amsterdam police resorted to firing live rounds of ammunition, resulting in nine dead and more than a hundred injured. Ration cards were introduced in an effort to calm the populace and restore order. And, as new supplies arrived the following day, peace was restored to the capital.■

07

05 Another Van Gogh-like scene: potato-pickers near Nuenen

Boiled potatoes

TRY ME →

An indispensable component of a true Dutch meal.
For crumbly potatoes. Peel the potatoes and cut them into equally sized pieces. Put them in a pan with a teaspoon of salt and just enough water to cover them. Bring the water to the boil with the lid on the pan. Continue to simmer the potatoes over a low heat for twenty minutes until done. Pour off the remaining water and allow the potatoes to steam. Shake them about in the pan once or twice while steaming.

one-pot cooking

NO FOOD EMBODIES TRADITIONAL DUTCH CUISINE BETTER THAN *STAMPPOT*, A SIMPLE DISH OF POTATOES MASHED WITH VEGETABLES. *STAMPPOT* IS A SYMBOL OF SOBER- NESS, HARD LABOUR AND MODERATION. TODAY THIS MOST BASIC OF MEALS HAS BEEN ELEVATED TO THE STATUS OF *HAUTE CUISINE* IN MANY DUTCH GOURMET RESTAURANTS.

01

Until recently most Dutch nationals would proudly portray themselves and their people as no-nonsense and down-to-earth. Such descriptions are not based on false pretensions, but on a sober and minimalist disposition that originates from the harshness of their everyday existence in the past. The Dutch not only appreciate these values in their fellow human beings, but also in the food they eat.

Simple and straightforward

Traditional Dutch cooking was centred on one cooking pot. The scarcity of ingredients and shortage of fuel meant that each meal had to be prepared in more or less the same way: peeled potatoes in the bottom of the pot, a layer of vegetables on top, crowned with – if you could afford it – a horseshoe-shaped smoked sausage, the Dutch *rookworst*. All the housewife had to do was mash the cooked vegetables and potatoes together and hey presto, dinner was ready.

For generations the hard-working Dutch sat down to this hot meal every day at six p.m., which has been dinnertime for the typical Dutch family since time began. A simple and straightforward meal, guaranteeing a well-filled stomach.

Comfort food for winter days

The days of hard physical labour are over for most Dutch people. In the kitchen the single cooking pot has been replaced by a battery of pots and pans in various sizes, and the very latest in kitchen appliances. *Stamppot*, however, has not declined in popularity and is still considered the most important exponent of Dutch cuisine. *Stamppot* is classic winter fare. As soon as autumn comes around a taste for *stamppot* surfaces in the Dutch subconscious, only to fade away again with the first spring sunshine. *Stamppot* goes hand in hand with short winter days, snow and cold, and with another Dutch passion, long-distance skating.

TRY ME →

Stamppot with kale and Dutch smoked sausage

The most popular Dutch winter dish.

Ingredients (serves 4)

1 kg potatoes
500 g finely chopped kale
(*boerenkool* – a dark green leafy cabbage)
1 Dutch smoked sausage (*rookworst*)
a little milk
salt
pepper
pinch of nutmeg

You will need a thick-bottomed pan and a potato masher.

Preparation

Peel and quarter the potatoes, and put them in the pan. Add just enough water to cover. Place the kale on top of the potatoes and add the sausage. When the water boils, turn down the heat. Cook on a medium light for twenty minutes. Once the sausage is tender (prick with a fork), put it on a separate plate and mash the potatoes and kale together with a potato masher. Add the milk, salt, pepper and nutmeg. When the mash is nice and creamy, it is ready to serve. Garnish with the smoked sausage cut into thin slices or chunks.

Elevated status

Stamppot can be prepared with different kinds of vegetables, kale and endive being the time-honoured favourites. New and trendier recipes have evolved, like *stamppot* with Brussels sprouts. For the connoisseur there is nothing better than fresh home-made *stamppot*, but traditionally prepared *stamppot* is also available in numerous (delicatessen) shops, and supermarket shelves are crammed with ready-made versions.

The best evidence of the popularity or, as some see it, revival of *stamppot* is the number of restaurants that have the dish on their menu in one form or another. This is due in particular to top chefs in the many gourmet restaurants springing up all over the Netherlands, who are putting a lot of effort into refined experimentation and recreating the dish with their own personal touch. In their hands the simple meal of mashed potatoes and vegetables is evolving into genuine *haute cuisine*.

Hutspot

A spicier variation of Dutch *stamppot* is *hutspot*, a mixture of mashed potatoes, onions, carrots and meat, dating back to the eighty-year Spanish occupation of the Netherlands. The inhabitants of Leiden put up a strong resistance against their oppressors, holding out for several months.

An abandoned cooking pot containing the leftovers of *hutspot*, found in October 1574 by an observant civilian, proved to the people of Leiden that the Spanish soldiers were retreating. The liberation of Leiden was one of the first steps towards Dutch independence and masses of people in the city still eat *hutspot* on the 3rd of October every year in remembrance of their freedom. ∎

05 *Stamppot* with spinach

TRY ME →

Hutspot with rib of beef

The famous 'liberation of Leiden' variety of *stamppot*.

Ingredients (serves 4)

600 g spare ribs (*klapstuk*) or braising steak
3 dl water
1 to 1.5 kg potatoes
1 to 1.5 kg winter carrots
500 g onions
100 g butter or margarine
1 dl milk
a good pinch of salt

You will need a thick-bottomed pan and a potato masher.

Preparation

Bring the salted water to the boil and cook the spare ribs for about an hour. Meanwhile peel and quarter the potatoes, scrape and dice the carrots and cut the onions into rings. Add the potatoes, carrots and onions to the meat and bring to the boil. Allow to boil for thirty minutes until all the ingredients are cooked. Take the meat out of the pot and keep it warm. Pour off the water from the potatoes and vegetables into a bowl for later use. Mash the potatoes, carrots and onions and mix together well. Boil the milk with the butter or margarine and stir into your *hutspot*. If the mash is too dry you can add a small amount of the cooking water you saved. Cut the meat into small pieces and stir into the mash.

Stamppot is classic winter fare. As soon as autumn comes around a taste for *stamppot* surfaces in the Dutch subconscious, only to fade away again with the first spring sunshine.

05

Europe's greatest veggie fans

VEGETABLES ARE *HOT* IN HOLLAND. THEY ARE ONE OF THE PRIME COMPONENTS OF THE MAIN DAILY MEAL AND ARE EVEN EXPERIENCING SOMETHING OF A REVIVAL. MANY 'FORGOTTEN VEGETABLES' ARE ONCE AGAIN FINDING FAVOUR IN DUTCH KITCHENS. WATCH OUT, THE ORIGINAL DUTCH BEETS ARE COMING!

01

The Dutch are one of the few Europeans who eat cooked vegetables every day. This healthy habit began around 1850, when new kitchen tools and methods of preparation pushed simple, one-pan-style casseroles onto the figurative back burner. The fertile Dutch soil provided plenty of produce for the new needs and tastes, and today a huge variety of vegetables decorate Dutch fields. And what won't grow in the open air will undoubtedly flourish in the vast greenhouses of the region called the Westland.

Vegetable pulp

People were always aware of the positive nutritional aspects of eating vegetables, but until recently cooked their potential vitamin source to a pulp. Beans were considered inedible unless they were boiled until completely soft.
These days, the Dutch cook knows that such preparation is akin to throwing the baby out with the bathwater; all the vitamins and minerals are lost into the cooking water. As a result, cooking times have become considerably shorter, and people steam, microwave and 'wok' their veg like there's no tomorrow.

New hope for the sprout

The different varieties of cabbage, endive, green beans and carrots are among the most widely consumed vegetables in the Netherlands. Among the brassica, cauliflower is an all-time favourite. A plate piled high with boiled potatoes, a meatball in gravy and cauliflower with cheese sauce is a Dutch classic. But, as with the other brassicas, there's always an unpleasant smell attached to cauliflower. Brassicas draw sulphur from the soil as they grow, which is released during the cooking process, leaving a penetrating odour. Before range hoods were commonplace, the pervasive smell would fill the house, causing the unsuspecting visitor to reach for his handkerchief.
The smell of Brussels sprouts, which were particularly popular in the 1950s, was sickening. The malodorous sprout with its bitter taste fell into disrepute for years. In Dutch vernacular, being in possession of a *spruitjeslucht*, the scent of boiled sprouts, is synonymous with harbouring narrow-minded views.
One Dutch seed company is set on rectifying the

reputation of the Brussels sprout by cultivating a new strain of sprout that has a sweeter taste and does not give off the unpleasant odour so commonly associated with this vegetable. In this way, it hopes to give the sprout a new lease of life. This should not be too difficult, since sprouts and other typically Dutch vegetables are in the process of being rediscovered, both by *cordon bleu* chefs as well as by average households.

Sprouts and other typically Dutch vegetables are in the process of being rediscovered.

TRY ME

Red cabbage with apples

The sweet flavour of the cabbage is intensified by the apples.

Ingredients (serves 4)

1 red cabbage	2 tsp cinnamon
1 dl vinegar	2 sweet apples
100 g soft brown sugar	

Preparation

Remove the outermost leaves from the cabbage. Slice the cabbage with a heavy knife into thin strips and then cut these into small pieces. Alternatively, you can shred the cabbage. Wash the cut or shredded cabbage and place it in a large pan with very little water. Add vinegar, sugar and cinnamon. Simmer the cabbage until it is soft and well cooked. Peel the apples and slice them thinly. Simmer the apple slices with the cabbage for a few minutes more. Stir the cabbage and apples thoroughly before serving, adding more sugar if required.

Sauerkraut: scurvy saviour

Sauerkraut, a popular winter staple when served with potatoes and sausage, is not an unadulterated gift from the ground, but is made from finely sliced white cabbage that is salted and left to ferment in a vat for several weeks. Sauerkraut can be bought packaged, but Dutch gourmets prefer to serve it fresh from the vat.

Eighteenth-century doctors acclaimed sauerkraut as the saviour of public health. It was an efficacious remedy for scurvy, a disease resulting from vitamin C deficiency and one that claimed many victims, especially in the winter.

Queen Asparagus

Positioned at the other end of the vegetable spectrum is the asparagus, reverently called 'white gold' or 'the queen of vegetables'. As with the season's first herring catch, people eagerly anticipate the first asparagus harvest. Once it has been harvested it is served simply, with hard-boiled eggs and ham. Even though this elegant vegetable grows well in all parts of the country, the southern province of Limburg is particularly well-known for its asparagus. A couple of years ago, at the beginning of asparagus season, a crop duster flew over the asparagus fields of Drouwerveen in the northern province of Drenthe, 'anointing' the fields with white wine. This was not just for symbolic reasons, but was also a stunt to promote asparagus cultivation in the North.

Forgotten vegetables

Taking a good look at the assortment of vegetables available in Dutch shops today might lead one to be-

03

04

08

lieve that shoppers have less choice now than in the past. Today's consumers use their eyes rather than their taste buds when making a choice. They are of the opinion that vegetables should be of a crisp green, snow white or deep red colour, and potatoes should have a brown skin and be slightly yellowish on the inside. Something as bizarre as a blue potato will be viewed with suspicion, and greens that have gone brown will usually lead them to complain to the store manager.

The Society for Forgotten Vegetables was founded a few years ago to remind people of the many forgotten vegetables. According to the Society, there are no less than seventy forgotten or near-forgotten kinds of vegetables, such as the parsnip, the original Dutch beetroot, Buggenummer Muuskes potatoes, burdock root, thistly cardoon and Edzell Blcu, the blue potato.

The Society's activities centre around the cultivation of forgotten vegetables, preserving their cultural and historical heritage and promoting their culinary secrets. The vegetables are cultivated on a small scale and used in authentic Dutch dishes.■

A plate piled high with boiled potatoes, a meatball in gravy and cauliflower with cheese sauce is a Dutch classic.

03 Most Dutch kids have an aversion to sprouts **04** Hothouse cultivation in Bleiswijk. The surrounding area, the Westland, is the largest greenhouse farming area in the world. Vegetables, fruit and flowers, mainly for export, are grown in the 'glass city' **11** Harvesting sprouts in the Schermerpolder

01

healthy and colourful

THE DUTCH LOVE THEIR VEGETABLES AND ARE FANATIC ABOUT SALAD, EATING IT BOTH AS A SIDE DISH AND A MAIN MEAL. RESTAURANTS WILL ALWAYS SERVE SALAD AS A 'SECOND VEGETABLE'. AND THERE IS NO LACK OF VARIETY. MANY DIFFERENT TYPES OF LETTUCE AND OTHER SALAD VEGETABLES ARE GROWN IN THE NETHERLANDS.

02

Part of the salad's popularity is due to the fact that it is both easy to prepare and full of vitamins. In winter, salad is usually served as a side dish, to accompany more wholesome, filling fare. But in summer, when temperatures rise and the Dutch begin to crave food that is easy to digest, Dutch chefs come into their own and create a huge variety of meal-sized salads.

Because there is such a rich variety of salad vegetables on offer in the Netherlands, it doesn't take long to prepare a healthy and nutritious meal. The main guideline is: the more colourful the salad, the more healthy it is likely to be. With this general rule of thumb in mind, the Dutch use more and more ingredients – the assortment is growing all the time – to aid their creativity.

Edible flowers

Salad eating became popular in the Golden Age, a time when both the culture and economy of the Netherlands flourished. In this period, the 17th century, it was even customary to add edible flowers, such as marigolds, nasturtiums, violets and rose petals to a salad. Olive oil, used widely in those days, as well as vinegar and salt were used to bring the flavour out. If olive oil wasn't available, butter was used instead, an alternative that remained in use well into the 20th century.
Of all the different varieties of lettuce, cabbage lettuce (its mild flavour lending it the nickname 'butter lettuce') is the most well-known, and a traditional accompaniment to a meal of steak with fried potatoes. The crunchier iceberg lettuce however, beats it in the popularity stakes. Its neutral flavour makes it the ideal basis for a healthy main-dish salad, especially when combined with cucumber, tomato, red pepper, hard-boiled eggs and slices of cheese.

Donkey's ears

The more bitter leafy salad ingredients, while very tasty, are not quite so popular. Parents, in particular, are reluctant to use them. Nonetheless, dandelion leaves and curly endive are slowly gaining ground amongst salad-lovers. The trick when using these more bitter varieties is to combine them with ingredients that take away some of the bitterness.

Dandelion leaves, which have a distinctive flavour, are an acquired taste and beginners are advised to start with young plants, and combine the leaves with small pieces of fried bacon. Fried bacon also combines well with curly endive. The traditional dressing for this salad uses melted blue cheese. If you want to avoid the bitter varieties altogether, there is still a lot of choice: oak-leaf lettuce, with its mildly nutty flavour, Dutch lamb's lettuce (*ezelsoren* or 'donkey's ears') and rocket. All of these combine well with fruit, nuts and eggs, but are also delicious with just a simple dressing.

One of the latest stars to appear on the Dutch salad horizon is *mosterdsla*, 'mustard lettuce', which, as its name implies, tastes of mustard.

A riot of colour

The number of lettuce varieties in the Netherlands has risen considerably in the last few decades. One of the latest stars to appear on the horizon is *mosterdsla*, 'mustard lettuce', which, as its name implies, tastes of mustard. And alongside the Dutch varieties, more and more imports from abroad are arriving on the scene, such as Roman lettuce and *roquette*, a French variety of rocket.

But the classics remain popular. Batavia lettuce for example, the predecessor of the iceberg, and *Amsterdams vet*, a lettuce variety with tiny leaves, are both still eaten widely.

Not all types of lettuce have that characteristic fresh green colour. Chicory, also known as Belgian endive, owes its whiteness to the fact that it is cultivated in a dark environment, while raddichio and oak-leaf lettuce have distinctive dark-red leaves. There is even a strain of lettuce with flamed, red-and-white leaves, obtained by crossing chicory and raddichio. Like chicory, it is often eaten raw, with raisins, sunflower or pumpkin seeds, apple and a yoghurt dressing. Chicory however remains most popular prepared in the oven, with ham and cheese.

07.

(two to three dessertspoons), the vinegar wisely (one dessertspoon), and the salt as though you're a spendthrift (one teaspoon)'.

When making the vinaigrette, it's important to first whisk the salt into the vinegar until it dissolves completely, and only then add the oil. Finally, herbs provide flavour: choose from dill, lemon balm, basil, celery leaves, parsley, thyme or chives. ■

Dressing up

The word 'salad' stems from Roman times, as does the custom of dressing salads with a sauce. The Dutch traditionally dress their salads with vinaigrette, a mixture of oil, vinegar and salt. There's a special recipe for achieving the right proportions: 'Use oil as though you're a squanderer

06

TRY ME →

Oak-leaf lettuce salad with blue cheese and pear

A hearty salad with a mildly nutty flavour.

Ingredients (serves 4)

1 head oak-leaf lettuce (around 200 g)	2 tsp mustard
	salt
75 g blue cheese	pepper
1 pear	4 dessertspoons olive oil
1 dessertspoons lemon juice	25 g peeled walnuts

Preparation

Wash and dry the lettuce and tear the leaves into small pieces. Cut or crumble the cheese. Peel the pear and cut into segments; sprinkle with some of the lemon juice. Whisk the remaining juice, together with the mustard, salt, pepper and oil into a dressing. Toss the lettuce in the dressing and sprinkle with the cheese. Decorate with walnuts and pear.

an apple a day...

DESPITE THE WEALTH OF EXOTIC FRUITS AVAILABLE IN SHOPS, THE DUTCH ARE NOT NATURAL FRUIT EATERS. THEIR LUNCH-BOXES MAY CONTAIN AN APPLE, AND THEY WILL ALWAYS HAVE A WELL-FILLED FRUIT BOWL ON THEIR TABLE, BUT THIS DOES NOT MAKE THEM GREAT FRUIT FANS. A FRUIT PIE, HOWEVER, IS ALWAYS APPRECIATED.

01

02

Fruit does not play a prominent role in Dutch agriculture. Of all the fruit grown in the Netherlands, apples and pears are by far the most important, and apples account for more than half of the total acreage. It's no surprise therefore that the country boasts hundreds of orchards. Most of the apple orchards are in the provinces of Gelderland, Utrecht, Flevoland, Zeeland, North Brabant and Limburg. Pear producers can be found mostly in Gelderland, Utrecht and Zeeland.

Specialist skill

In the old days, farmers kept just a few fruit trees that they tended in their spare time. 'An apple a day keeps the doctor away', as the old saying goes. These days, fruit growing is a specialist skill amongst some 2,300 farms and businesses in the Netherlands. Small-scale orchards with tall trees can still be found here and there, but the demands placed on modern agriculture for efficiency have resulted in endless hectares of uniformly pruned, short trees.

Pick of the crop

Sweet, tart, large and small. Dutch apples are harvested in an assortment of sizes, colours, aromas and flavours. Harvesting starts in July and August with the firm-fleshed James Grieve, Discovery and Alkmene, amongst others. Varieties such as the Elstar and

In an effort to influence its subjects' eating habits, the government launched a campaign to encourage people to eat more fresh fruit. Two servings a day, at least.

Cox's Orange are harvested in autumn. Dutch pears are available all year long. They can be divided into dessert pears and stewing pears, but within these two groups there are many different varieties, all with evocative names. First to be harvested are Holland Clapps, Triomphe de Viënne and Doyenne du Comice. The stewing pears St. Remy and Gieser Wildeman follow shortly after.

Going pear-shaped

To be honest, Dutch people are remarkably uncon-cerned about the value of fresh fruit, despite the considerable effort that has been put into changing their minds. Dentists were the first to try, with the motto 'Snack sensibly, eat an apple'. But the man in the street didn't seem to advance much further than the daily apple in his lunch-box.

In an effort to influence its subjects' eating habits, the government launched a campaign to encourage people to eat more fresh fruit – two servings a day, at least. The campaign however bore little fruit, but it did result in initiatives in some parts of the country to persuade at least schoolchildren to eat more fruit. According to experts, Dutch people are simply not accustomed to eating fruit on a regular basis, and good habits such as these need to be taught at a very young age.

So do Dutch people ignore fruit altogether? Absolutely not. But their favourite way to eat fruit is as part of a sweet dish or product. Apple sauce, apple spread, fruit yoghurt, jam, stewed pears, strawberries with cream, fruit pies and, last but certainly not least, the much-lauded Dutch apple pie are all favourites.

And if all these sweet products threaten the waistline, then the Dutch simply reach for a good old-fashioned dessert pear, which is said to have slimming and diuretic properties. ∎

TRY ME

Traditional Dutch apple pie

'Granny's apple pie', as it is made for generations.

Ingredients

For the crust	For the filling
175 g sugar	12 small- to medium-sized
250 g real butter	cooking apples
2 eggs	cinnamon
pinch of salt	sugar
500 g self-raising flour	150 g currants or sultanas

Preparation

Peel and quarter the apples, slicing each quarter thinly. Place the apple slices in a bowl, add two heaped des-sertspoonfuls of sugar, sprinkle with cinnamon and mix well. Soak the currents or sultanas in warm water, rinse in a sieve and drain.
Pre-heat the oven to 190° C. Grease a 28 cm-diame-ter spring form and sprinkle it lightly with flour. Mix together the sugar, butter, eggs and salt to a smooth consistency. Sift the self-raising flour into the dough and knead until it no longer sticks to the hands. Cover the base of the spring form entirely with dough and press down firmly. Now press more dough around the sides of the spring form, making sure that it sticks well to the pastry on the base. Cover with a layer of apple slices, overlapping them, and sprinkle a handful of currants or sultanas on top. Repeat. Make strips from the rest of the pastry and lay them on top of the pie in a criss-cross pattern. Brush with whisked egg yolk, to add an attractive sheen, and bake for fifty minutes until golden brown and cooked through.

03 Apple orchard in Enspijk **04** Strawberries, affectionately called 'summer kings', are considered a treat in summer **05** Apple harvest at the fruit nursery Vereecken in Dronten

DOWNLOADING_HERRING ▶

ESTIMATED TIME 1.28 MIN .

STEP TWO

SELECT ONIONS

DOWNLOADING 15.9%

STEP THREE

TAKE POSITION

DOWNLOADING 32.7%

STEP ONE

BUY HERRING

DOWNLOADING 6.4%

CUTTING

CUTTING

meat

01

Being full-blooded carnivores, for many Dutch people meat is the most important component of the daily hot meal. In the watery country the Netherlands is, fish is also very popular. Among it the famous snack detested by many foreigners, raw herring with onions.

A SMALL EDIBLE FISH WITH SILVERY SCALES THAT LIVES
IN LARGE SHOALS IN THE NORTH ATLANTIC AND IS COMMERCIALLY
VERY IMPORTANT TO THE AREA'S FISHING INDUSTRY.
LATIN NAME: CLUPEA HARENGU

STEP FOUR

START DOWNLOADING

DOWNLOADING 57.1%

STEP FIVE

ENJOY

DOWNLOADING 86.3%

CUTTING

CUTTING

STEP SIX

LOSE TAIL

DOWNLOAD COMPLETE

& fish

CAUTION

AFTERWARDS USE SOME MINTS FOR FURTHER SOCIAL ACTIVITIES.

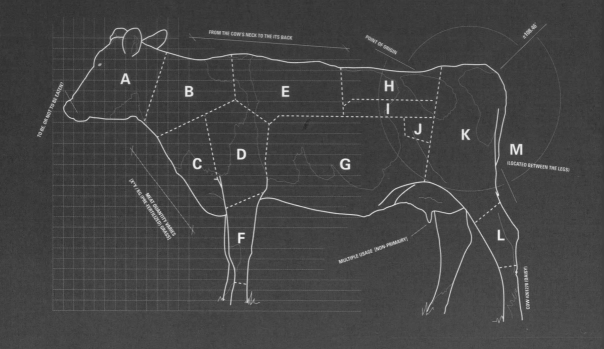

Diagram labels:
- TO BE OR NOT TO BE EATEN?
- FROM THE COW'S NECK TO THE ITS BACK
- POINT OF ORIGIN
- ±108.46°
- A
- B
- E
- H
- I
- J
- K
- M
- (LOCATED BETWEEN THE LEGS)
- C
- D
- G
- F
- L
- (X+Y) KG (PRE-FERTILIZED GRASS)
- MEAT QUANTITY VARIES
- MULTIPLE USAGE (NON-PRIMAIRY)
- COW #261278 (DAISY)

01

# of sausages and meatballs

FOR MOST DUTCH PEOPLE, MEAT IS THE MAIN INGREDIENT OF THE DAILY HOT MEAL. VEGETABLES AND POTATOES, OR RICE, ALSO HAVE THEIR PLACE, BUT ARE LESS IMPORTANT THAN STEAK, PORK CHOPS OR MEATBALLS. THE AVERAGE DUTCH PERSON IS A FULL-BLOODED CARNIVORE.

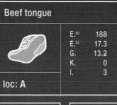

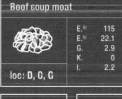

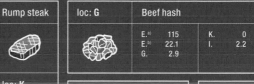

loc: C — Marbled braising steak
- E.a) 188
- E.b) 19.9
- G. 12.1
- K. 0
- I. 2.5

Frying steak
loc: D, K
- E.a) 108
- E.b) 22.6
- G. 1.9
- K. 0
- I. 1.6

Beef tongue
- E.a) 188
- E.b) 17.3
- G. 13.2
- K. 0
- I. 3

loc: A

Shin of beef
- E.a) 113
- E.b) 22.6
- G. 2.6
- K. 0
- I. 2

loc: F, L

loc: C — Marbled beef roulade
- E.a) 126
- E.b) 22.5
- G. 4
- K. 0
- I. 2

Rump steak
loc: G

loc: G — Beef hash
- E.a) 115
- E.b) 22.1
- G. 2.9
- K. 0
- I. 2.2

Beef soup meat
- E.a) 115
- E.b) 22.1
- G. 2.9
- K. 0
- I. 2.2

loc: D, O, G

Beef liver
- E.a) 124
- E.b) 20.7
- G. 3.6
- K. 2
- I. 7

loc: J

loc: K
- E.a) 109
- E.b) 23.8
- G. 1.5
- K. 0
- I. 2

Hamburger
- E.a) 234
- E.b) 19.1
- G. 17.6
- K. 0.8
- I. 2.4

loc: D, D, G

Entrecote
loc: H
- E.a) 145
- E.b) 22.8
- G. 6
- K. 0
- I. 2.5

Roast beef
loc: K
- E.a) 122
- E.b) 22.9
- G. 3.4
- K. 0
- I. 2.1

loc: B, D, G — Minced beef
- E.a) 234
- E.b) 19.1
- G. 17.6
- K. 0.8
- I. 2.4

loc: D — Thin sliced slivers of beef
- E.a) 108
- E.b) 22.6
- G. 1.9
- K. 0
- I. 1.6

Beef sausage
- E.a) 234
- E.b) 19.1
- G. 17.6
- K. 0.8
- I. 2.4

loc: B, D, G

loc: E — Stewing steak from the rib
- E.a) 171
- E.b) 20.8
- G. 9.7
- K. 0
- I. 2.5

Tournedos
- E.a) 109
- E.b) 23.8
- G. 1.5
- K. 0
- I. 2

loc: I

Oxtail
loc: M
- E.a) 113
- E.b) 22.6
- G. 2.6
- K. 0
- I. 2

Mince wrapped in schnitzel
- E.a) 212
- E.b) 20
- G. 14.1
- K. 0
- I. 2.5

loc: B, D, G

Rib of beef
loc: G
- E.a) 166
- E.b) 20.4
- G. 9.4
- K. 0
- I. 2.5

Beef schnitzel
- E.a) 109
- E.b) 23.8
- G. 1.5
- K. 0
- I. 2

loc: D, K

Lean stewing steak
- E.a) 129
- E.b) 20.9
- G. 5.1
- K. 0
- I. 2.5

loc: D

Round steak
- E.a) 109
- E.b) 23.8
- G. 1.5
- K. 0
- I. 2

loc: K

Rib-eye steak
- E.a) 145
- E.b) 22.8
- G. 6
- K. 0
- I. 2.5

loc: E

Steak tartar
- E.a) 127
- E.b) 21.8
- G. 4.4
- K. 0
- I. 2

loc: B, D, K

loc: H — Beef loin roulade
- E.a) 126
- E.b) 22.5
- G. 4
- K. 0
- I. 2

loc: D — Lean braising steak
- E.a) 108
- E.b) 22.6
- G. 1.9
- K. 0
- I. 1.6

Tenderloin
- E.a) 116
- E.b) 23.7
- G. 2.3
- K. 0
- I. 2

loc: I

{E.a) Energy + E.b) Eggwhite + G. Grease + K. Koolhydrates + I. Iron} = 'nutritional value per 100 grams unprepared'

Indeed, the majority of Dutch people eat meat every day, the type of meat depending on their budget and the day of the week. Traditionally, Wednesdays were always 'mince' day, largely because on that particular day mince was always on special offer at the local butchers.

Game for all sorts

The Dutch eat all kinds of meat, from pork chops, *slavink* (a kind of meatball wrapped in bacon) and veal schnitzel, to beef stew, steak, hash and mince. Smoked sausages and pork crackling are also popular. And for the strong at heart, old-fashioned *balkenbrij*, a kind of offal sausage made from pigs' heads, blood and liver, is a special treat.

The Dutch have always been big meat eaters, and, especially in the past, when they ate meat, they ate a *lot* of meat.

Meat, however, was held in higher regard in the past than it is today, enjoying a far superior status to vegetables for instance. The Dutch have always been big meat eaters, and, especially in the past, when they ate meat, they ate a *lot* of meat. When hunting was still commonplace in the Netherlands, they ate mostly game. A deer or wild boar was usually roasted and served whole.

Other than game, which is not so widely eaten these days, the Dutch were also fond of fattening pigs and other 'free-roaming' farm animals, which, according to common belief, produced better meat than animals kept in stalls. These days, the Dutch still prefer pork to beef.

Let them eat cake!

The preference for pork is underscored by the popularity of smoked sausage (*rookworst*), which gets its name and characteristic flavour from a brief smoking treatment in a special oven. Dishes such as curly kale stew [SEE PAGE 35] and pea soup [SEE PAGE 26] are simply not complete unless they're served with a juicy smoked sausage.

However, one type of smoked sausage is often enjoyed on its own: the Hema sausage. Hema's chain of department stores sells its sausages hot and ready to eat in a small bag that invariably leaks grease. Leaving a trail of greasy fingers and smiling faces, Hema smoked sausage is a regular treat on many a shopping trip.

Smoked sausages do have to be served hot. In the east of the country, the Twente Sausage Society became livid when the local Hema announced that their sausages would have to be eaten cold in future. The Society's members announced a boycott of the store, only to be lifted if the decision was revoked. This somewhat playful crusade hit the national papers, and Hema invited the protesters to their store for coffee and sweets, saying 'Let them eat cake!'

Mash and meatballs

Smoked sausage can be prepared at home in no time, but the same can't be said for all meat dishes. Beef stew, for example, has to simmer for at least two hours before the meat is tender enough to literally fall apart.

Beef stew comes straight out of 'grandmother's kitchen', as does the Dutch meatball. But one big difference between the two is that it is almost impossible to make a bad meatball. A few herbs and a pinch of stray spice are used to liven it up a bit,

but what makes the meatball so characteristically Dutch is the gravy that always accompanies it. A simple sauce made from the juices of the meat, gravy is as important to the Dutch as the meat it is made from. Indeed, try to get through all those plain boiled potatoes without it and you'll see why. The gravy makes them soft and palatable.

Gravy is made in the same pan in which the meat has been cooked. Water is added to the fats and shreds of meat left in the pan. Add a little salt and pepper, stir well, and the gravy is done. Those with a bit of imagination will replace the water with milk, cream, bouillon, wine, sherry, brandy or other spirits, or add a bit of curry powder or paprika. The traditional way of eating your mash and meatball is to mash the potato with your fork, use the gravy ladle to make a well in the middle of your potato puree, fill it with gravy and let the meatball nestle into it.

A term of abuse

As with some other common dishes, the Dutch meatball has been added to the list of terms hurled at others by way of abuse. If someone does something really foolish, he is quite likely to be called a 'meatball'.

Steak will never suffer such humiliation. It has always been held in higher regard than the meatball and used to be the exclusive reserve of the well-to-do. Until recently, steak was only eaten in regular Dutch households on special occasions or to fortify the sick. Most Dutch people prefer their steak cooked medium, and usually garnish it with one of various sauces. ■

04 Top-quality butcher Frans van Vuuren in Utrecht 05 Free-range pigs in Gemert 06 Gnawing away at the carnival, Maastricht 2005 07 A butcher smoking meat

---

TRY ME

Beef stew A famous beef dish, which needs at least two hours of simmering.

Ingredients (serves 4)

500 g stewing beef (sukadelappen)
fat or oil for frying
salt & pepper
paprika powder
5 cloves
2 tomatoes
1 slice of bread
1 dessertspoon mustard
2 bay leaves
1 bottle of beer

Preparation

Cut up the beef into chunks. Quarter the tomatoes. Spread the bread thickly with mustard. Heat oil or cooking fat in a heavy-bottomed pan. Sear the chunks of meat on all sides until sealed. Add salt, pepper and paprika. Reduce heat by half and add tomatoes, cloves and bay leaves. Add the beer and lay the bread on top. As soon as the liquid starts to boil, reduce the heat and allow the beef to simmer for at least two hours, checking regularly to make sure the meat, bread or herbs are not sticking to the pan.

watery country, fishy kitchen

THE DUTCH LANDSCAPE IS A WATERY NETWORK OF LAKES, RIVERS AND CANALS TEEMING WITH FISH, MANY OF WHICH END UP ON THE TABLE. THE DUTCH LOVE FISH, AND VISITORS WILL BE ABLE TO ENJOY A RANGE OF FISH SPECIALITIES, FROM RAW HERRING WITH ONIONS FROM A STREET STALL TO COUNTLESS INSPIRED CREATIONS.

FISH

The Dutch are surrounded by water. A quarter of their country lies below sea level, and about twenty percent of their land has been reclaimed from the sea. Indeed, it is a miracle they don't have fins of their own. Obviously fishing has always played a major role in Dutch subsistence. The lives of the inhabitants of numerous fishing villages such as Urk, Marken, Volendam, Katwijk, Noordwijk and Yerseke revolved around fish for centuries. Even those not working in the fishing industry itself found employment in related trades.

Fishing villages

While the North Sea was teeming with herring, cod and mackerel, the South Sea, or IJssel Lake as it is now called, was the place to fish for anchovies, flounder, eel and also herring. The IJssel Lake was cut off from the open sea by an enormous dyke to control recurrent flooding, but for the local fishing population this was bad news. Luckily the typical characteristics of the fishing villages were preserved. They have now become hugely popular tourist destinations, famous not only from a folkloric point of view but also for their excellent fish restaurants.

Raw, poached and deep-fried

The Dutch eat a lot of fish, and not only because of its alleged health benefits. Dutch people love rich food, and one of their favourite dishes is a simple one: a battered and deep-fried fillet of cod. The most popular Dutch fish snack is raw herring with onions (SEE PAGE 57). Other fish, such as haddock, sole, pollack, and salmon, are generally poached and served 'swimming' in a creamy sauce, while fillet of sole and plaice are preferred fried.

With a quarter of their country lying below sea level it is a miracle the Dutch don't have fins of their own.

01 Shrimp fisher at work on the Wadden Sea **02** Crates full of shrimps **03** Fishing boat near Colijnsplaat **04** Women in traditional costume on a dyke near Scheveningen **05** Sign at a merchant house called De Drie Haringen ['The Three Herrings'] in Deventer, built in 1575

TRY ME ➡

Eel in green sauce

A Dutch speciality for the fish devotee.

Ingredients (serves 4)

1 kg eel, gutted and cleaned
50 g butter
30 g fresh parsley
30 g fresh chervil
30 g fresh sorrel
15 g fresh tarragon
1 bay leaf
4 fresh sage leaves
2 dl of dry white wine
1 dl cream
2 egg yolks
0.5 tsp of thyme
salt & pepper
1-2 tbsp of lemon juice

Preparation

Cut the eel into chunks. Heat thirty gram butter and brown the eel on both sides, then lower the flame and cook through in about fifteen minutes. Finely chop the parsley, chervil, sorrel and tarragon. Melt the rest of the butter, crush the bay leaf into it, add the sage and allow to fry for a minute. Add the wine and the cream, bring to the boil and simmer for about five minutes on a low flame. Sieve the sauce. Beat the egg yolks with a little warm sauce and add this mixture to the rest of the sauce. Stir in the chopped herbs and thyme and warm the sauce right through (but don't allow to boil again). Season with salt, pepper and lemon juice. Pour the sauce over the fried eel just before serving.

Although fresh fish is by far the tastiest, more and more people are resorting to the frozen alternative. Preferably filleted, for who has time to fiddle with fish bones over dinner these days? And while connoisseurs enjoy delicacies like shrimp croquettes, the more common fare of fish fingers, which come in various shapes and sizes, is often served to children as their first taste of fish.

Eels and shellfish

Another typical Dutch dish is smoked eel. An amazing six million kilos of eel are smoked every year in the Netherlands. More than half of these are filleted, the rest are sold in one piece and may end up in the fish sandwiches sold from market stalls and in fish shops.
The Dutch shrimp and the Zeeland mussel and oyster are the most popular varieties of shellfish eaten in the Netherlands. The North Sea shrimp differs from other types in colour and size and has a very distinct flavour. The Dutch enjoy their shrimps, immersed in cocktail sauce, as a sandwich filling.

The one that got away...

'Neither meat nor fish' is a Dutch expression meaning 'neither one thing nor the other'; indeed, something quite different. And if you order the local dish of 'Kamper sturgeon' in the province of Overijssel that is just what you will get. Despite its name this dish does not consist of a cooked sturgeon, but of eggs in mustard sauce.
The recipe for this meal was invented to replace a colossal sturgeon, which was supposed to be cooked and served to a very important guest. When the guest postponed his visit at the last moment the sturgeon was thrown back into the sea with a bell around its neck in the hope it would be easy to find when it was needed. Of course it was never caught again, and at the last minute an alternative dish had to be served: a 'sturgeon' of eggs and mustard.

Slippery sounds

Yet another misleading term is 'eel sound'. This has nothing to do with the sound an eel makes, but is the name given to the popular musical genre introduced many years ago by several bands from the traditional fishing village of Volendam. Bands such as *The Cats* and *BZN* had a huge following at home and abroad, amongst both fish-lovers and fish-haters. ∎

07 Example of the famous 'eel sound': the single *Marian* from *The Cats*, released in 1969

HERRING

the salty Dutch 'mate'

WHILE THE MERE IDEA OF EATING RAW FISH MAKES MOST FOREIGNERS FEEL QUEASY, THE WAY THE DUTCH DO IT IS ENOUGH TO PUT YOU OFF FISH FOREVER. HOLDING THE RAW HERRING BY ITS TAIL, THEY 'DOWNLOAD' THEIR FISH, TILTING THEIR HEADS BACK AND LETTING IT SLIDE IN SLOWLY.

01

TRY ME →

Haringhappen, or The Fine Art of Herring Consumption

Keep your eye out for a herring vendor, who could be selling his wares from a bicycle, a street stall or a small kiosk in a shop-lined street. Look out for the words *Haring* or *Hollandse Nieuwe*, accompanied by a bunch of Dutch flags.

Approach the herring vendor as if you do this every day. Beware of appearing apprehensive. Whatever you do, don't giggle. Be cool.

Now try to pronounce the word correctly: *haaa-rrrring*; the *a* as in *lava*, with the emphasis on the first syllable. The vendor will resume his conversation with whoever he was talking to before you appeared while laying the herring onto a cardboard tray or plastic plate.

Just before he hands it over, he will look up and ask: '*Uitjes?*' Reply in the affirmative – '*ja*' (yes) – and your herring will be garnished with a spoonful of freshly chopped onion.

Now, still in your Dutch act, accept the herring and prepare for 'download'. Lift the fish by its tail, allowing some onion spill. Take a subtle deep breath, open your mouth as wide as you can and tilt your head back. While holding the herring by its tail, lower it into your mouth. Sink your teeth in, chew the soft flesh, swallow swiftly and take another bite in the same pose until you reach the fish bones near the tail. Don't feel you have to eat them! You don't want the vendor to have to reach over and pull them out of your throat.

When you're done, clean your fingers with one of the napkins on the counter. Say that it was good ('*goed*', pronounced with the guttural *g*, a bit like the *ch* in *loch*). Oh, and don't forget to pay.

Dutch people like their herring, and they like it raw. And with all that water around, that is hardly surprising; they've had herring coursing through their veins for centuries. References to herring consumption date back to 1000 AD. The Netherlands, with its fleet of several hundred herring boats, has always played an active role in the North Sea herring fishery, but it took a long time for the little fish to come into its own.

Gutting the herring

Growth in the herring fishery was hindered by the fact that the fish didn't remain fresh for long. In fact, the delicacy could really only be enjoyed by those living in or near fishing villages.

People were eager to find a way to keep the fish fresh for longer, and in 1380 a man by the name of Willem Beukelsz thought up the process of *haring-kaken*, or gutting the herring. A razor sharp knife is used to partially gut the fish in one well-aimed slice.

Because of this new process the herring fisheries grew at an explosive rate. The gutting took place on board of the ships, which meant that the fishermen could stay at sea longer. Thanks to this new method of preservation, herring soon became available all over the country.

From fish to icon

From that point on, herring became something of a national dish, making regular appearances in the country's history and its local traditions. In Leiden for example, herring is served with white bread every year on the 3rd of October, to commemorate the retreat of Spanish troops in 1574, during the Eighty Years' War.

Herring also plays a prominent role on Flag Day, *Vlaggetjesdag*, when an annual herring race is held. On the last Saturday in May, herring boats sail out from the harbours of Scheveningen and IJmuiden to start the hunt for the year's new herring catch. The first vessel to return with the much-praised *Hollandse Nieuwe* wins this prestigious contest. The first barrel of new herring is auctioned, usually fetching a handsome price.

How raw is raw?

Visitors to the Netherlands usually maintain a safe distance from herring – until they've tasted it. This initial aversion usually has to do with the fact that Dutch herring is eaten raw. But just how raw is raw? By gutting the herring, salting it and then freezing the fish it is in fact subjected to a slow maturing process that affects both taste and tenderness. So

Many visitors to the Netherlands are turned off by the way Dutch people grab the herring by its tail and slowly let it slide into their mouths, biting off tasty morsels as they go.

the fish is not really raw in the strictest sense. Furthermore, the Dutch feel that eating the fish in its raw state is much healthier than cooking it, because the nutrients are preserved. Herring contains lots of beneficial fats and fatty acids, which have a positive affect on the circulatory system. However, whether this is enough to sway the wary visitor is doubtful. It's not just the apparent rawness that makes them sceptical, but also the traditional 'heads first' way in which the Dutch devour their favourite delicacy. Many visitors to the Netherlands are turned off by the way Dutch people grab the fish by its tail and slowly let it slide into their mouths, biting off tasty morsels as they go.

But if you can't be persuaded to immerse yourself in tradition to this extent, you can always choose to eat your herring from a plate, cut into bite-sized pieces and consumed with a little flagged cocktail stick. The liberally minded Dutch do tolerate this slight deviation from tradition. ∎

01 Successful integration: tourist consuming a raw herring the classical way at the Albert Cuyp market in Amsterdam 03 Poster promoting the consumption of herring 06 Herring vendor at the Prinsengracht in Amsterdam, an ideal spot to practice the fine art of *haringhappen*

desserts

01 Women in Scheveningen, dressed in traditional costume, enjoying a *bakkie*, a cup of coffee

& coffee

Having a sweet tooth, The Dutch love sweet desserts. The most popular dessert is *vla*, or Dutch custard, a product unknown outside the Netherlands. And the evening meal wouldn't be complete without at least one cup of coffee.

saving the best for last

IT MAY NOT BE OBVIOUS TO THE CASUAL OBSERVER, BUT THE DUTCH HAVE A SWEET TOOTH. THEIR FONDNESS FOR ALL THINGS SUGARY IS EVIDENCED BY THE LARGE NUMBER OF DUTCH DESSERTS, WHICH FORM THE 'ICING ON THE CAKE' OF ANY MEAL. SOME DESSERTS ARE SO RICH THAT PRECEDING COURSES ARE LITTLE MORE THAN FOREPLAY.

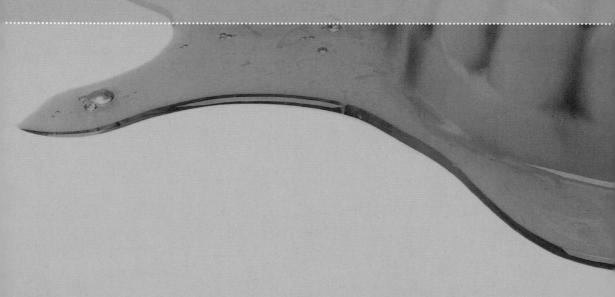

01

When it comes to their first course, the Dutch generally plump for a modest soup. Their main course will be substantial and nourishing. But when it's time for dessert, they lose their self-control and give in to any one of a number of tempting desserts that might appear on the table.

Some of these are light and airy, others rich and filling – it doesn't really matter as long as they're sweet. The Dutch enjoy their *vla* (SEE PAGE 65), cakes, chocolate mousse, strawberries and cream, *crêpes*, ice cream or any of the other staggeringly sweet desserts, like no other.

The icing on the cake

The Dutch have a weakness for desserts. They are the high point of any meal, eagerly anticipated during the other courses and a good reason to clean their dinner plate in a timely fashion. Even if the main course fails to live up to expectations, a pleasing dessert will make up for any disappointment. Old-fashioned cookery books divide desserts into two broad categories: those that serve as a small but flavoursome conclusion to a meal, and those, more filling, that are made from grains. The Dutch are particularly fond of the latter.

For the heavyweights

Foreigners are often amazed by the richness of Dutch desserts, but the Dutch take it in their stride. From semolina pudding with fruit juice, cold rice pudding with apricot compote, warm rye pudding with vanilla sauce, sweet oatcakes, grits with prunes – all grain-based desserts go down equally well.

Some desserts are light and airy, others rich and filling – it doesn't really matter as long as they're sweet.

Most of them are made from corn or other grains, cooked in milk and then sweetened with syrup or sugar. Many different ingredients can be used to put the finishing touch to these, leading to endless variations on a common theme.

Semolina pudding, made from milled durum wheat cooked in milk, has been a popular Dutch dessert for centuries. These days, supermarkets offer it packaged and ready to eat, complete with a portion of the requisite red berry juice.

Rice pudding, another firm favourite in the pudding repertoire, is also available pre-packaged in the shops, as are macaroon and chipolata pudding. In fact, there are so many ready-to-eat grain puddings available that slaving over a hot stove to make these hearty desserts is hardly a priority in Dutch households nowadays.

02 *Watergruwel* (water gruel), a dessert consisting of yoghurt, red currants and currant juice **03** A new look for an old-fashioned dessert: semolina pudding with strawberry juice

Haagse bluf

Haagse bluf is an evergreen in that other category of desserts, those that form a more modest closure to a meal. Similar to currant whip, *Haagse bluf* (literally 'The Hague bluff') owes its name to the reputation enjoyed – or suffered – by citizens of The Hague, where the dessert originated. Their compatriots outside of the city often regarded them as boastful and self-important, not least because of the way they appeared in public, always dressed to the nines. This local dessert, while appearing rather volumi- nous, is in fact nothing more than a few spoonfuls of whipped egg white and red berry juice. In other words, it appears to be more than it is, as do the fine citizenry of The Hague with their posh attitudes and distinguished demeanour. At least, according to their detractors.

But the origins of its name in no way detract from the appeal of *Haagse bluf*. However, it is important to eat this dessert quickly, because the berry juice can cause the meringue to collapse. *Haagse bluf* is delicious when served with ice-cream or yoghurt. ▪

Haagse bluf owes its name to the reputation enjoyed – or suffered – by the citizens of The Hague.

04 *Haagse Bluf* (literally 'The Hague Bluff')

TRY ME →

Jan in de Zak (John in the Bag)

An old-time cake, simply too delicious to resist.

Ingredients

For the cake	For the syrup
200 g flour	2 dl milk
10 g baker's yeast	20 g flour
or 5 g dried yeast	75 g syrup
1 cup lukewarm milk	40 g butter
5 g salt	
150 g currants and sultanas	
1 egg	

Preparation

Rinse the currants and sultanas and leave them to drain. Combine the yeast with some of the warm milk and set aside. Mix together the flour and salt and make a well in the middle. Break the egg into the flour, add the yeast mixture and the rest of the milk and stir from the inside out to make a smooth batter. Mix in the cur- rants and raisins. Cover the batter and let it rise in a warm place for 45 minutes. Coat the inside of a muslin bag (or large tea towel) with flour, and spoon the batter into the bag. Close the bag, leaving enough room for the mixture to rise. Place a plate upside-down in a pan of water and bring the water to the boil. Now place the bag on top of the plate in the boiling water and let it simmer for about ninety minutes. When done, remove the cake from the bag and let it cool in a warm place.

For the syrup

Add enough milk to the flour to make a smooth, lump- free paste. Dilute it further by adding a little more milk. Bring the rest of the milk to the boil and add the paste, stirring constantly. Stir in the butter and syrup and serve the sauce warm with slices of cake.

04

the most popular pudding

VLA, OR DUTCH CUSTARD, IS BY FAR THE MOST POPULAR DUTCH DESSERT. UNKNOWN OUTSIDE THE NETHERLANDS, EVEN THE SMALLEST OF SUPERMARKETS WILL STOCK A LARGE ASSORTMENT OF FLAVOURS, EACH ONE SWEETER THAN THE LAST.

01

TRY ME →

Vanilla *vla*

The first Dutch *vla*, and still a favourite of many.

Ingredients (serves 4)

1 l milk	50 g sugar
1 egg	1 vanilla pod
50 g corn starch	pinch of salt

Preparation

Break the egg into a mixing bowl, add the sugar and salt and whisk together. Stir in the corn starch. Put the milk in a saucepan together with the vanilla pod, and bring slowly to the boil, allowing the vanilla to flavour the milk. Remove from the heat. Stir the milk into the whisked egg mixture, then pour back into the saucepan. Stirring constantly with a whisk, let the *vla* simmer on a low heat for three minutes. Remove the vanilla pod and allow the custard to cool. Stir occasionally to prevent the formation of a skin.

Vla's basic ingredient is milk. It is made by heating the milk, then adding corn starch and sugar. This forms an ideal basis for the further addition of flavourings such as vanilla, cocoa, whipped cream, caramel, fruit juices and bitter-macaroon. After the flavouring has been added, the mixture is heated again, causing it to thicken and all the ingredients to blend together to a smooth consistency.

Packaged and ready to pour

Vla can be bought ready made in cartons. Indeed, it would probably surprise the younger generation to know that until a few decades ago, *vla* was often made at home. The preparation is simple, but it requires a great deal of attention, otherwise the *vla* will boil over and you'll have to start all over again. If it was up to the dairy industry, those days are gone forever. Today, customers are constantly given new flavours to try, all of them packaged and ready to pour. The first *vla* to appear in the shops was vanilla, and this remains one of the most popular varieties. But these days it faces stiff competition from chocolate, toffee, caramel, stracciatella, macaroon, banana, whipped cream, and the so-called white custard (*blanke vla*) variety.

02

The latest *vla* variety, banana flavour with added chocolate chunks, opens the way for a whole range of possibilities, guaranteed to keep the Dutch sweet for quite some time.

The flip trip

Vla is particularly good when eaten with fruit and yoghurt, a fact that the dairy industry took advantage of when launching a new product a few decades ago. *Vlaflip*, a mixture of concentrated fruit juice, custard and yoghurt, was introduced to the country through commercials which presented the new dessert as a mathematical formula: syrup plus custard plus yoghurt equals *vlaflip*. The colourful combination of red strawberry syrup, yellow vanilla custard and white yoghurt not only looked attractive, but tasted good too, which landed *vlaflip* squarely in the dessert top-ten.

With the introduction of new custard flavours, *vlaflip* declined in popularity. Today the flip is still available ready made, but real dessert fans enjoy experimenting with the proportions themselves. For them, the only real flip is the homemade flip.

Keeping the customer sweet

As the *vla* assortment in the shops continued to grow, the dairy industry almost ran out of new ideas. Almost. They hit on *dubbelva*, a combination of two flavours, and two colours, in one pack.

This was a double treat for dessert-lovers. Today they can enjoy vanilla/caramel, chocolate/vanilla and banana/strawberry combinations. As with the custard flip, the colours are not unimportant. *Dubbelvla* is not only tasty, but also a treat for the eye. The advent of *dubbelvla* led to further creative opportunities. It wasn't long before red-and-white 'football' *vla* appeared in the shops, a combination of white and strawberry *vla*. Supporters of the most successful and popular Dutch teams, Ajax, Feyenoord and PSV, were for a while able to demonstrate their allegiance by their choice of *vla*. However, success was short-lived; 'football' *vla* hasn't been spotted in the supermarkets for some time. Another variety, which only appears in the shops on special occasions, is *oranjevla*, or orange *vla*. Orange is the colour used to denote both the Dutch royal family (the House of Orange) and the Netherlands' national football team. *Oranjevla* is made on the occasion of the Queen's birthday (a national holiday in Holland), a royal birth, or when the Dutch football team is taking part in a big tournament.

The dairy industry is steering a new course with

01 *Vlart*, or vla-art, designed by Dutch Publishers. Ingredients: caramel *vla*, Bolino (vanilla *vla* with chocolate chunks), chocolate *vla*, white *vla*, strawberry *vla*, banana *vla*, orange *vla*, syrup, *hagelslag* (chocolate sprinkles), Smarties, chocolate rods and macaroons **02** The famous *vlaflip*

its latest *vla* variety: banana flavour with added chocolate chunks. This opens the way for a whole range of possibilities, guaranteed to keep customers sweet for quite some time.

Yoghurt takes a back seat

In spite of their predilection for sweet *vla*, the Dutch also enjoy yoghurt and *kwark*, a kind of soft curd cheese made from skimmed milk. Their popularity can be put down partly to their health-giving qualities. Yoghurt can even be bought in low-fat, sugar-free and low-calorie varieties.

When eaten as a dessert, the addition of fruit, fruit juice, compote, and cream and sugar makes them extra tasty. But as sensible and flavoursome as they may be, yoghurt and *kwark* take a back seat compared to *vla*, Holland's firm favourite. ∎

'wrong' coffee and Senseo

THE DUTCH EVENING MEAL WOULDN'T BE COMPLETE WITHOUT AT LEAST ONE CUP OF COFFEE TO ROUND IT OFF. AND IT'S NOT JUST IN THE EVENING THAT THE COFFEE FLOWS FREELY. WHATEVER THE TIME OF DAY, WHEN THE DUTCH GET TOGETHER, COFFEE WILL ALWAYS BE SERVED: BLACK, WITH SUGAR OR WITH LASHINGS OF HOT MILK.

COFFEE

01

The Dutch love their coffee. They drink, on average, three cups a day, that's 142 litres a year. The first cup is a 'wake-up' cup; the second, usually drunk at around ten in the morning, is a pick-me-up, and the third they enjoy after their evening meal.

Of course there are millions of Dutch people who take every opportunity they can to drink coffee – business meetings throughout the country will unearth the real addicts. But coffee drinking is usually associated with the typical Dutch phenomenon *gezelligheid*, or conviviality. Drinking coffee is largely a social activity. If the Dutch want to get to know someone better, they will invariably ask him to 'drop by for coffee'.

What's wrong?

While the social ingredient is top of the agenda on such an occasion, the coffee is far from unimportant. The Dutch believe that the main purpose of coffee is enjoyment, and they always enquire how visitors like their coffee: strong or weak, with sugar only, milk only, or 'with everything you've got', i.e. sugar and a dash of cold milk.

The word *verkeerd* means 'wrong', so it's hardly surprising that the term *koffie verkeerd* confuses many a visitor. 'Wrong coffee? What's wrong with it?'

And then there's that typically Dutch variation *koffie verkeerd*, a large coffee made with hot milk. The word *verkeerd* means 'wrong', so it's hardly surprising that the term *koffie verkeerd* confuses – and amuses – many a visitor. 'Wrong coffee?' they enquire. 'What's wrong with it?' But it's a term that's understood in cafés and restaurants throughout the country, and these days the personnel are equally familiar with foreign variations such as cappuccino and espresso.
Decaffeinated coffee is also quite common in the Low Countries, but has never really caught on. It is regarded as a pointless imitation of the real thing, with no flavour and little in common with real coffee, which keeps the Dutch going all day, every day. 'Decaf is for wimps', is the broadly held attitude.

Trends and traditions

While Dutch coffee drinkers firmly uphold their traditions, they are also open to new trends. Indeed, there are few other nations that take to

01 Grand café at the concert hall De IJsbreker in Amsterdam **02** The Senseo coffee machine, made by Philips **03** Served at the Dutch coffee shop: cannabis **04** One of the first 'coffee machines' made by famous coffee producer Douwe Egberts **05** 'Coffee is being served'

EEN EN AL GEUR EN SMAAK!

Douwe Egberts
Aroma Koffie

Koffiebranderijen

D·E ROOD·MERK

DOUWE EGBERTS
JOURE EN UTRECHT

DOUWE EGBERTS

D·E

ANNO 1753

DOUWE
EGBERTS
KOFFIE

new methods of coffee preparation as quickly and readily as the Dutch. The oldest way of preparing coffee is to pour hot water onto finely ground coffee beans. The disadvantage with this is that it leaves dregs, forcing the drinker to leave a full mouthful of their precious coffee at the bottom of their cup. But the advent of filter coffee and the automatic coffee-maker soon did away with dregs. Nearly every Dutch kitchen boasts an automatic coffee-maker. It is, however, a controversial machine. Purists maintain that its glass jug should be washed with water alone. This, they argue, will ensure that the full flavour of fresh coffee remains in the jug, adding to the flavour of every subsequent cup. Not everyone agrees. The latest rage to hit the Dutch coffee market is the hugely popular Senseo from Philips. Pads replace the traditional filter papers, enabling a cup of freshly made coffee to be made, literally, in a minute.

Coffee houses and coffee shops

Coffee has been a firm favourite with the Dutch since the 17th century, when the renowned Dutch East India Company brought coffee beans into Holland from the Dutch East Indies, present-day Indonesia. Coffee was regarded as a luxury, served only in coffee houses. However, the service didn't please everyone. On one particular night in 1670, the coffee house in The Hague was wrecked by enraged customers, horrified to learn that the establishment no longer served hot coffee.

When coffee houses started serving spirits, they changed their name to *café*, the French word for 'coffee'. But there are two types of establishments serving coffee that never adopted this title. The first of these is frequented largely by Turkish and Moroccan men, who seek out each other's company over small cups of strong black coffee. The other, the 'coffee shop', is a smoky establishment where the aroma of coffee is disguised by that of other mind-altering substances: hash and marijuana.

...and then there's tea

Compared to coffee, the popularity of tea is currently at a low. Up until the Second World War, tea was more popular than coffee. It was *hot* in both senses of the word, and made with the devotion usually lavished upon it by the English. The tea-leaves were contained in a tea-ball, hung inside the pot. The teapot was kept warm under a thick tea cosy with a silver snap fastening, a typically Dutch invention, rarely seen anymore. Apart from the introduction of the tea bag, little has changed in the tea-making process itself. What has changed is the choice of teas available in Dutch tea caddies. Where there used to be just one type of tea on offer, there are now several sorts of black tea as well as fruit teas, herb teas and green tea. And where the tea cosy used to take pride of place on the Dutch tea table, it is now only used by those reluctant to relinquish the last traces of nostalgia, made redundant by insulated teapots and single-cup tea-bags. ■

06 Old advertisement for Douwe Egberts coffee

TRY ME

Dokkumer Coffee (*Dockumer Kofje*)

The Frisian version of Irish Coffee.

Ingredients (serves 4)

1 l milk	50 g sugar
1 egg	1 vanilla pod
50 g corn starch	pinch of salt

Preparation

Whip the cream and sugar together until almost stiff. Put two teaspoons of brown sugar in a large glass and add the slightly warmed Berenburg (SEE PAGE 76). Add the hot coffee to the mixture and stir well. Pour the cream over the rounded side of a spoon onto the coffee. Sprinkle with candied sugar or a little brown sugar.

01 *Jenever* distillery De Ooievaar in Amsterdam

drinks

The Dutch invented the process of distillation and treated the world to *jenever* (Dutch gin) and dozens of bitters and other liquors. The national drink, however, is beer. Nowadays the Dutch brewery Heineken treats the world to its famous clear pilsner.

dutch gin and bitters

WHEN IT COMES TO SPIRITS, THE NETHERLANDS HAS QUITE A REPUTATION TO MAINTAIN. THE DUTCH WERE THE FIRST TO TURN DISTILLATION INTO A FINE ART. THEY INTRODUCED THE WORLD TO *JENEVER*, DUTCH GIN, AS WELL AS DOZENS OF BITTERS AND OTHER LIQUORS. THESE DAYS, DUTCH VODKA IS A BIG HIT IN THE STATES.

01 & 02

By the end of the Middle Ages, the Dutch were already pioneers of the distillation process. In the 16th century the world's first commercial distillery opened its doors in Amsterdam. Even before then, the drinking of highly alcoholic *brandewijn* (which is where the word 'brandy' originates) was commonplace in the Low Countries. Brandy was the preferred tipple at any special occasion. To celebrate the birth of a child, for example, *kandeel* (caudle) was served, made from brandy, sugar and eggs.

The distillation of alcohol is as old as the search for eternal youth. In the case of *jenever* the two practices are said to be linked. *Jenever*, which gave Dutch distillers international fame, takes its name from the juniper berries (*jeneverbessen*) used in its preparation. The berry is said to have rejuvenating qualities.
However, rejuvenation was not the primary goal of those early distillers. Their main concern was to find a remedy for all kinds of illness. Malt spirit formed the base of their concoction. It was made from grain and had a powerful aroma. Herbs were added to help disguise the bitter taste.
A learned Dutch doctor of the day infused the malt spirit with juniper berries, believing that *juniperus* (the Latin term for 'juniper berry') possessed youthful energy that would help the body fight disease.

01 & 02 Courtesy of Bols - www.bolscocktails.com **03** Antique *jenever* glass **04** A glass of liqueur **05** Stylish décor for a drink: grand café Polmanshuis, Utrecht **06** Giveaway from Dutch airline KLM: Bols *jenever* in a 'canal house' bottle **07** Collection of Dutch booze in restaurant De Vijf Vliegen in Amsterdam **08** Mr Hooghoudt, former owner of the famous Hooghoudt distillery

After distillation, the drink was dubbed *jenever* and praised as a preventative medicine for all sorts of ailments, including the plague. According to the wisdom of the time, only a few drops were needed for optimal results. But the prescribed dose left the patient wanting more. The medicine soon became a drink imbibed more for pleasure than anything else.

Bitters for the jitters

By refining their distillation methods, and experimenting with common herbs such as aniseed, fennel and caraway, the Dutch soon began producing their famous bitters. The enormous popularity of these medicinal drinks led to the old saying 'a mouthful of bitters drives out the jitters'.
Intensive international trade soon meant that Dutch distilling methods, and their famous bitters, could be found all over the world. English gin, for example, is a variation on *jenever*. And using sugar cane to distil rum was also a Dutch invention. Even a number of French cognac houses were founded by the Dutch.

Berenburg and haddock brine

From time immemorial, bitters have been especially popular among Dutch seafarers. In the 19th century, Frisian captains sailing from the north to the bulb fields in the w est of the land, were the largest buyers of herb mixtures, which they purchased from a famous spice merchant named Hendrik Beerenburg. They infused wine, brandy and *jenever* with the herbs and enjoyed them to the full, convinced of their health-giving qualities.

One of Beerenburg's regular customers was an innkeeper named Fedde Sonnema. He came up with the brilliant idea of infusing *jenever* with Beerenburg's herbs, plus a few additions of his own, and letting the mixture stand for a full day. The result was a reddish-brown drink that soon became popular with the locals, especially those seafaring skippers. Business pressures forced Sonnema to share his recipe with Beerenburg, who then began supplying all of the herbs for the drink. Sonnema graciously named the drink after the spice merchant, but, to leave his mark, left one *e* out of the name.

Berenburg still is the most well-known bitter, but other bitters sold well too. Fishermen from the town of Vlaardingen brewed a drink that they called *schelvispekel*, or 'haddock brine'. In the galleys of the haddock boats, there was always a bowl filled with herbs steeping in brandy. The fishermen used the drink to help ward off the cold at sea. As with Berenburg, *schelvispekel* is now available all across the country.

The rise of Dutch vodka

However, *jenever* seems to have had its day. The younger generation now regard it as an 'old man's drink', preferring cocktails and other fashionable drinks, leading distillers to look at alternatives. One of their successes is vodka, which is being distilled and sold with success by several distilleries.

Abroad, the reputation of Dutch *jenever* remains untarnished. In Ghana, for example, births, marriages, funerals and even parliamentary elections all call for a libation, and the drink of choice for pleasing the spirits is traditional Dutch *jenever*.

In keeping with tradition, most *jenever* is still distilled in the town of Schiedam, near Rotterdam. Once, there were more than four hundred distilleries in operation in Schiedam, also the birthplace of Ketel One, the vodka that has won over trend-conscious America. Few of Ketel One's fans know that the drink originates not in Russia, but in the Low Countries.∎

Jenever **was praised as a preventative medicine for all sorts of ailments. Only a few drops were needed, but the patients wanted more.**

09 Windmill De Nieuwe Palmboom, one of twenty giant mills in Schiedam that once milled the grain needed to make *jenever*. Five of those still exist. De Nieuwe Palmboom houses the Spirits Museum De Gekroonde Brandersketel **10** Traditional preparation of *jenever* in the Spirits Museum

TRY ME

Holland Razor Blade

A pungent cocktail, based on *jenever*.

Ingredients (serves 2)

2 shot glasses *jonge jenever*	ice
1 shot glass lemon juice	cayenne pepper

Preparation

Mix together the *jenever* and lemon juice in a cocktail shaker. Add ice cubes and a dash of cayenne pepper. Shake, don't stir. Serve in cocktail glasses.

09

10

symbol of enjoyment

BEER IS THE NATIONAL DRINK OF THE NETHERLANDS. TO THE DUTCH, SOCIALIZING AND UNWINDING ARE INEXTRICABLY LINKED WITH THE DRINK. AND DUTCH BEER IS JUST AS POPULAR ABROAD. HEINEKEN IS ONE OF THE WORLD'S LEADING BEER PRODUCERS, WITH THE CLEAR HEINEKEN PILSNER AVAILABLE IN OVER 170 COUNTRIES.

To the Dutch, a glass of golden beer with a good head on it is synonymous with enjoying the company of others and relaxing. Whenever Dutch people get together, in the pub, café or at home, beer is part and parcel of the pleasant atmosphere. A glass of beer symbolizes the feeling of contentment and togetherness that is so cherished by the Dutch.

The Dutch beer of choice is pilsner (or lager), which is also the most famous beer in the world. Pilsner is brewed in a specific way and, with its alcohol percentage of 4.5 to 5.5, is classified as a strong beer. The name comes from the Czech town of Plzen, where it originally comes from.

A breakfast beverage

The fact that beer has become such a popular drink in the Netherlands dates back to the great bubonic plague and cholera epidemics of the 14th century. In an attempt to stop the spread of these diseases, a ban was imposed on drinking the contaminated water from the canals, rivers and ditches. Beer was considered a safe alternative as the brewing process gets rid of all health-endangering bacteria in the water.

In the days before breweries, the beverage was prepared by women and monks. People drank a light beer in the morning, which they even used to make their porridge. In the evening a stronger type was

served. For children there was a special children's beer and even sick people and pregnant women were given beer. Hop, beer's main ingredient, helped the sick to regain their appetite and gave pregnant women an energy boost.

Heineken, a household name

Beer can be brewed in many different ways. The oldest technique involves the use of top fermentation, in which the type of yeast the brewer uses influences the character, smell and flavour of the beer. The major disadvantages of this method are that it is impossible to determine the flavour in advance and that the beer spoils quickly.

Louis Pasteur's experiments with different strains of yeast and his discovery that by preheating you can preserve a beverage for longer, opened new doors for beer brewers. In 1870, Amstel was the first Dutch brewery to start using brewer's yeast. The famous Heineken brewery soon followed suit. This set the stage for a fierce competitive rivalry between the two breweries, from which Heineken eventually emerged the winner.

Heineken's 'working man's beer' became renowned at home and abroad and was given the honorary name of *herenbier* (gentleman's beer) in the Netherlands. Heineken was also the first brewery to start exporting its beer, and the Dutch brand has become a household name all over the world. Heineken is one of the

TRY ME ➜

Hot beer

A spicy alternative to a cold pilsner.

Ingredients (serves 2)

1 l beer	rind of half a lemon
1 dl rum or brandy	2 eggs
cloves	125 g brown sugar
10 cm cinnamon stick	a pinch of salt

Preparation

Heat the beer on a low flame and allow to stand for a while with the spices and the lemon peel. Beat the eggs and sugar in a bowl. Pour this mixture into the spicy beer. Do not allow the liquid to boil. Take the pan off the heat and add the rum or brandy.

largest breweries worldwide and the leading beer exporter. The beer is sold in 170 countries.

Other Dutch beers

In fact Heineken beer is so famous that some people have come to regard the brand as synonymous with Dutch beer. But the Amstel brewery, which was taken over by Heineken in 1975, also produces a reputable beer that is served in no less than ninety countries in the world. Other Dutch breweries include Grolsch, with its distinctive swing-stopper bottle, Brand, which is also under the Heineken umbrella now, Bavaria, Dommelsch and Hertog Jan.

Though pilsner is the most popular, the Dutch also enjoy other types of beer. *Bokbier*, for example, brewed from each year's new corn harvest, and Trappist beer, which was originally brewed in Benedictine monasteries. This sweet dark brown beer is very suitable for cooking and tastes good with spicy food. Fruit beers, made of fruit extracts, juices and syrups, are favoured amongst a certain group of beer-lovers.

Four basic flavours

Beer is one of the few beverages that encompasses the four basic flavours; it is at once sweet, sour, salty and bitter. Malt sugar makes it sweet, carbonate makes it sour, minerals give it its salty edge and hop adds the bitterness. Confirmed beer drinkers are convinced of the nutritional value of a glass of beer,

01 The world famous green Heineken bottle **02** Beer being served at café d'Pley in Noorbeek **03** The Grolsch swing-stopper bottle **04** The Heineken Experience (Brewery Museum) in Amsterdam **05** Grolsch stoppers waiting for a bottle at the ultramodern Grolsch plant in Enschede **06** Outdoor café in Leiden **07** Even the medics drink beer at the carnival

which they say is comparable to one slice of wholewheat bread.

Despite this claim, however, the consumption of beer has been dwindling somewhat in the past few years. While the Dutch were drinking an annual 85 litres of beer per person a few years ago, this average has now fallen to eighty litres. The reason for this decline is the growing popularity of other drinks, such as the many sweet mixes on the market, as well as rosé wine and cocktails. Beer, however, remains the one drink that the Dutch associate with the feeling of contentment and togetherness they call *gezelligheid*.

Beer museum

Beer-lovers with a special interest in Dutch beer can learn more about the brewing process and other particular aspects of the drink in locations all over the Netherlands. Visit the Heineken Experience, for example, in Amsterdam's former Heineken brewery, or take a trip through the history of beer brewing in the National Beer Museum De Boom in Alkmaar. Wind up in the museum's pub to make a closer acquaintance with the many types of beer that are brewed in the Low Countries. ∎

regenboog-lolly
€ 1.--

handjessnoepen
€ 3.50

discostok
€ 2.50

3.

01 Sweets stall at a fairground in Oosterhout. Fransiscus Bul, born in 1905, is an old hand in the sweets business

sweets

82→ drop
86→ marsepein 2→
90→ treacle waffles
92→ biscuits, cakes and cookies

Walk into any supermarket or, even better, a Dutch sweet shop, and you will immediately become aware that the Dutch have a sweet tooth. The shelfs are crammed with an amazing assortment of sweets and biscuits. Among them famous specialities such as the irresistible treacle waffle and the black liquorice sweet *drop*.

dropstok

wijnstok
€ 2.-

black gold

WHY ARE THE DUTCH SO PASSIONATE ABOUT *DROP*? MOST FOREIGNERS ASSOCIATE THE TASTE OF THE LIQUORICE SWEET WITH MEDICINES AND ILLNESS. IT'S AN ACQUIRED TASTE, APPARENTLY, AND YOU HAVE TO STICK WITH IT IF YOU REALLY WANT TO GET INTO THE DUTCH NATIONAL SPIRIT. OR YOU COULD JUST DROP THE WHOLE ISSUE.

DROP

The Dutch and their liquorice are inseparable. A lot of people can't stand the taste of this black sweet, but the Dutch chew and suck their way through mountains of the stuff. Statistics show that over thirty million kilos of liquorice are consumed every year in the Netherlands, costing a total of 150 million euro. Topping the list of national favourite liquorice sweets, or *drop*, is the classic *muntdrop*: coin-shaped, hard and sweet.

Medicinal *drop*

Nobody knows just how or when this national penchant for liquorice started. The two main ingredients of the liquorice sweet, liquorice root and Arabic gum, have been used far and wide throughout history to soothe coughs and sore throats. While Napoleon was known to distribute liquorice sweets amongst his troops as a thirst-quencher, the use of the liquorice root dates back to Ancient Egypt, as suggested by remains found in Pharaoh Tutankhamen's tomb. Based on old Sanskrit writings we also know that liquorice root has been used in India for centuries as a base in the preparation of medicines. It is this medicinal quality of liquorice, which is still used in cough medicines today, that most non-Dutch nationals dislike so much about *drop*. They associate that somewhat bitter taste with illness.

...and even a drop to drink

They've got the wrong end of the stick, however. To the Dutch, being ill or having a sore throat is exactly the excuse they need to throw all caution to the wind. Encouraged by supermarket shelves stocking liquorice right next to the cough sweets,

05

the slightest hint of a frog in the throat has people consuming huge amounts of *drop* – enough to make anyone sick – or preparing themselves a *drop grog*, a strong mix of liquorice syrup and Dutch gin.

Confirmed sweet tooths – sore throat or not – will invariably have some *drop* tucked away in their coat pocket, bag or desk drawer. Liquorice keeps them company as they work, helps them bond with their colleagues, gets them through a dull moment and plays a role in the children's upbringing. They even keep a stash on the bedside table, just in case they wake up in the middle of the night with a craving.

If you look into the suitcase of any Dutch traveller you are bound to come across the typical cone-shaped paper bag of assorted *drop*, all too often the source of deep suspicion from a foreign immigration officer who thinks he's found a hoard of black opium. Dutch nationals who work abroad often have a hard time doing without, and beg the home front for mailings of *drop* to alleviate their homesickness.

01 & 04 Liquorice shop the Drop Inn in Utrecht **03** Liquorice

honingdrop
honey liquorice • Honiglakritze
pastille de réglisse au miel • regaliz de miel
liquirizia al miele • honungslakrits

100 g **0 80**

zwart & wit salmiak
black n white liquorice • Schwarz-Weiß-Salmiak
réglisse en forme d'ourson blanc et noir • regaliz blanco
y negro • liquirizia bianca e nera • svartvit lakrits

ZOETE BEERTJES ZWART WIT

0 25 by the small bag

zoute drop
salty liquorice • Salzlakritze
pastille de réglisse salée • regaliz salado
liquirizia salata • saltlakrits

100 g **0 80**

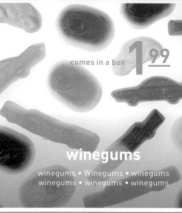

duimdrop
flat liquorice • Daumenlakritze
pastille de réglisse à sucer • regaliz de pulgar
liquirizia piatta • lakritsmatta

by the piece **1 15**

droplulletjes
liquorice willies • Lakritzenpimmel
réglisse en forme de phallus • regaliz de pichita
cazzetti di liquirizia • lakritssnoppar

comes in a small tin **4 50**

winegums
winegums • Winegums • winegums
winegums • winegums • winegums

comes in a box **1 99**

salmiakjes
diamond liquorice • Salmiak-Lakritze
diamants en réglisse • rombi di liquirizia
pastillas de regaliz con sal de amonio • Diamantlakrits

100 g **0 80**

katjesdrop
cat-shaped liquorice • Katzenlakritze
réglisse en forme de chaton • regaliz de gatito
gatti di liquirizia • lakritskatter

100 g **0 80**

muntdrop
coin-shaped liquorice • Lakritzengeld
pièce de monnaie de réglisse • regaliz de mone
monete di liquirizia • lakritsmynt

100 g **0 80**

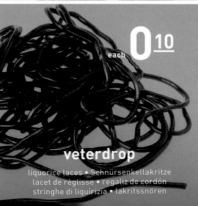

honingdrop
honey liquorice • Honiglakritze
pastille de réglisse au miel • regaliz de miel
liquirizia al miele • honungslakrits

100 g **0 80**

veterdrop
liquorice laces • Schnürsenkellakritze
lacet de réglisse • regaliz de cordón
stringhe di liquirizia • lakritssnören

each **0 10**

boerderijdrop
farmer-shaped liquorice • Bauernlakritze
pastille de réglisse en forme de fermier • regaliz de la
• gli abitanti della fattoria di liquirizia • bondlakrit

100 g **0 80**

laurierdrop

laurel liquorice • Lorbeerlakritze
réglisse au laurier • regaliz de laurel
liquirizia amara • lakritsblad

Manneken Pis

Manneken Pis liquorice • Manneken-Pis-Lakritze
anneken Pis en réglisse • Manneken Pis di liquirizia
Pastillas de regaliz salado Manneken Pis
Manneken Pis-lakrits

kokindjes

button liquorice • Knopf-Lakritze
pastilles de réglisse • bottoni di liquirizia
caramelos blandos de regaliz • Knapplakrits

dropshot

dropshot • Dropshot • dropshot
dropshot • dropshot • dropshot

Nipples and cannonballs

This delicious, seriously addictive, sometimes tiny and sometimes mouth-stopping black sweet comes in all sorts and sizes. But there are only two flavour variants: sweet and salty.

Sweet *drop* includes favourites like *duimdrop* (for liquorice-flavoured thumb-sucking), *trekdrop* (in strips), *kokindjes* (shaped like a nipple, according to some), *katjes* (cat-shaped), *dropruitjes* (sugar-coated squares), *Engelse drop* (a colourful assortment of liquorice and coconut-flavoured sweets) and *sleuteldrop* (key-shaped). Amongst the salty varieties are *boerderijdrop* (a liquorice farmer complete with farmhouse and farm animals), *jujubes* (diamond-shaped), *salmiakkogels* (a cannonball filled with acidic powder), *bielzen* (shaped like railway sleepers), and, for the true devotee, *dubbelzoute drop*: twice as salty.

Liquorice dick

Liquorice sweet manufacturers seem to have no trouble coming up with new types of drop. Flavour is only one important ingredient, for the shape also has to appeal, or at least stand out. Endless experiments with shapes and sizes have led to new additions to the assortment, like the *Manneken Pis* (in the shape of the famous Belgian statue of a little boy urinating) and even an edible penis, adding new meaning to the derogatory Dutch term for fool: *droplul*, or 'liquorice dick'.

> *Drop* comes in all sorts and sizes. There's even an edible penis, adding new meaning to the derogatory Dutch term for fool: *droplul*, or 'liquorice dick'.

While Dutch liquorice generally becomes sweeter, more and more people are opting for varieties that have a salt concentration rather similar to that of the Dead Sea. All in all, liquorice-lovers have never before enjoyed such diversity of their favourite sweet.

Alongside the classic varieties on the market we now find UFOs (with a slightly acidic flavour), *tikkels* (hard on the outside, sweet, salty or fruit-flavoured), *karameldrop* (chewy and caramel-flavoured), *salmiakriksen* (lighter-coloured coin shapes) and *bodemvondsten* (a 'treasure trove' of odd shapes).

Black gold

No matter what shape and flavour the end result, all liquorice is made in the same way. The basic ingredient is a thick, hardened pulp made of the ground-up and boiled-down roots of the liquorice bush. Once in the factory, slabs of this solid pulp are dissolved in water and mixed with gelatine, sugar, glucose syrup, starch and Arabic gum.

The resulting liquorice dough is then mechanically flavoured, boiled back into liquid form and poured into plaster moulds. After two days the liquid has solidified and the sweets are put through a polishing machine, emerging as the shiny black liquorice sweets the Dutch know and love so well – their very own 'black gold'. ■

sweet temptation

WHEN IT COMES TO EATING SWEETS, NOBODY BEATS THE DUTCH. THE CHOCOLATE BAR, KNOWN THE WORLD OVER, OWES ITS EXISTENCE TO THEIR UNBRIDLED APPETITE FOR CONFECTIONERY. THE DUTCH ARE PASSIONATE ABOUT THEIR SWEET-EATING, AND THERE ARE FEW SHOPS QUITE SO SEDUCTIVE AS A DUTCH SWEET SHOP.

01

And seductive is the word. Bowls of colourful candy greet the visitor on arrival, many of them filled, of course, with liquorice (SEE PAGE 82). There is chocolate in all shapes and sizes, as well as soft, yellow-and-pink marshmallows and bags of old-fashioned black-and-white *drop* with their pronounced flavour.

Equally delicious are the 'magic balls' that change colour as you suck them, and the dark red 'wine balls', so big that even the greediest kids have trouble fitting them into their mouths. And there are sticks of rock that can be licked for days on end. A selection to make your mouth water!

Champion sweet-eaters

It may seem as though such classics have been around for ever, but in the 17th century, sweets were limited to confections made exclusively from sugar. Amongst the elite, it was popular to present guests with a small gift of confectionery when they arrived. At the time, sweets were much too expensive for everyday budgets. Until a French chemist devised a method for extracting sugar from sugar beets. As a result, the production and consumption of sugary confectionery soared. Well-known Dutch companies such as Van Melle, Jamin, Verkade and Droste expanded their bakeries to include sweet factories. Droste's characteristic chocolate pastilles are as popular today as they ever were. Verkade also devoted itself to chocolate-making, while Van Melle tried its hand at other sweets such as acid drops. Jamin created a fashionable environment in which to display its bonbons and 'sweets of the week'. Confectionery gradually began to lose its elitist image, and slowly but surely the Dutch became the undisputed world-champion sweet eaters. On average, each Dutch citizen consumes six kilos of sweets a year, nearly two kilos more than any other European and five-and-a-half kilos more than even the most heavily addicted Asian.

Sought-after souvenirs

The thoroughly Dutch *drop*, or licquorice, is the most popular confectionery, but the Dutch also love anything even remotely related to chocolate. One characteristically Dutch bar of chocolate (a

02 Cinnamon and peppermint flavoured *kussentjes*, or cushions **03** The marshmellow variety called *spekkies* **04** *Haagse hopjes*, or Hague toffees

product thought up by the Dutchman Van Houten) is the so-called *koetjesreep*, or 'cow bar'. Instantly recognisable by its Delft Blue wrapper bearing an image of a black-and-white cow, it is hard to imagine anything more Dutch. Bonbons and other 'chic' chocolates are wrapped in an air of quality. Considered a special treat, they are often presented as a gift to one's hostess.

In the old days, it seems, people were partial to tougher sweets. Traditional treats such as pear drops, sticks of rock, wine balls, chewy nougat, *stroopsoldaatjes* ('molasses soldiers') and butter waffles can now only be found in speciality shops and at fairgrounds.

One type of confection that has virtually disappeared from the assortment is *jodevet*, the sugary leftovers that dripped off candy-making machines. Candy on a stick, the predecessor of today's lolly, is now used for sweetening tea, but one treat that has survived

intact is the *ijsbonbon*, or 'ice chocolate'; the wrapping usually bears a proverb or saying. Another old-fashioned treat, *Haagse hopjes*, are so popular that they have become sought-after souvenirs. The *Haagse hopje* was invented by a certain Baron Hop, resident of The Hague. One day, he noticed that the cup of mocha with sugar he had been enjoying had turned into a rather delicious, if very sticky, substance. Taking it to the local confectioner he had a batch of coffee-flavoured sweets made and the first 'Baron Hop's bonbons', which only later were christened *Haagse hopjes*, were born.

Spongy sweets

Other confection, popular with young and old, are the spongy, sweet varieties. *Tum-tum*, for example, is a mix of small, sugar-coated jelly sweets and tiny chocolates. *Spekkies* are tooth-curlingly sweet marshmallows. Tasting of vanilla they are usually sold in flat, pink and yellow diamond shapes. However, the dark grey liquorice-flavoured *spekkies* are also irresistible.

Eating sweets was once the privilege of the rich. Today, it is within everyone's reach. Indeed, chocolate bars such as Mars, Twix and Bounty are eaten more and more as a quick, between-meal snack. As a result, Dutch dentists are prospering.∎

05 *Boterbabbelaars*, or butter sweets **06** 'Small cow's' chocolate bar **09** *Zeeuwse boterbabbelaars*, or Zeeland butter sweets, a speciality of the province of Zeeland

07

← TRY ME

Chocolate rum truffles An exquisite Dutch delicacy.

Ingredients
(for ten truffles)

1.8 dl whipping cream
400 g plain chocolate
70 g butter
2 dessertspoons rum
cocoa powder or *hagelslag*
(chocolate sprinkles)

Preparation

Bring the cream to the boil in a saucepan. Remove from the heat and stir in the chocolate until melted. Add the butter and continue to stir until it melts. Now stir in the rum. Pour into a mixing bowl, cover and refrigerate for at least two hours or until stiff. Using about one dessert spoon for each truffle, take out spoonfuls and shape into little balls. Let them stiffen further in the fridge. Roll them in cocoa powder or *hagelslag* and shake off any excess. Keep in the fridge and allow them to reach room temperature before serving.

On average, each Dutch citizen consumes six kilos of sweets a year, nearly two kilos more than any other European and five-and-a-half kilos more than even the most heavily addicted Asian.

sticky and irresistible

THE TREACLE WAFFLE ONCE WAS AN EXCLUSIVE GOUDA SPECIALITY, BUT IS NOW
EXCEEDINGLY POPULAR ALL OVER THE NETHERLANDS. IN FACT THE WAFFLE IS SO
IRRESISTIBLE THAT EVEN THOSE WHO HAVE A HARD TIME TAKING TO OTHER DUTCH
TREATS LIKE *DROP*, INSTANTLY FALL IN LOVE WITH THIS STICKY SPECIALITY.

TREACLE WAFFLES

01

TRY ME

Treacle waffles

Ingredients (for ten waffles)

For the waffles	For the filling
250 g flour	600 g treacle
100 g soft brown sugar	300 g cane sugar
200 g butter	100 g butter
10 g yeast	0.5 tsp of cinnamon
1 egg	
pinch of salt	

You will also need a waffle iron.

Preparation

Sieve the flour into a bowl and slice the butter into the
flour using two knives. Dissolve the yeast in two tablespoons of warm water and stir into the flour, adding the
egg and the soft brown sugar. Knead the mixture into
a pliant dough and leave to rise for an hour. Bring the
treacle, the cane sugar and the cinnamon to the boil
while stirring, then simmer for ten minutes. Cut the butter into small pieces and stir into the treacle. Continue
stirring while the treacle cools and thickens into a paste.
Form small, slightly flattened balls of dough and place
between the tongs of the waffle iron to bake. Remove
the waffles from the iron, allow to cool a little and then
cut open. Quickly spread treacle on one side and close
up. Do not wait too long with filling; once the waffle has
cooled completely it will crumble under your knife.

Stroll through a market, fair or any other organised open-air event in the Netherlands and you are bound to come across a very popular Dutch treat: the treacle waffle. You will usually find the waffle vendor making fresh waffles in the tiniest of stalls, with just enough space for a couple of baking trays and mixing bowls. The smell of freshly made treacle is enough to make even the sturdiest Dutchman's mouth water, and the waffle vendor is rarely short of customers.

Biscuits for the poor

Treacle waffles are made from flour, sugar, eggs, salt, treacle and melted butter. The dough is rolled into small balls, which are flattened between the diamond-patterned tongs of a waffle iron and baked for about a minute. The waffle has to be sliced open while still hot, otherwise it will crumble. The two halves are then spread with treacle – a sticky substance made mainly from butter and soft brown sugar – and sandwiched together.

The treacle waffle was originally made from leftovers. It was first made in 1784 by a Gouda baker, who used up crumbs and spices to make a waffle and then filled it with treacle.

In the first years of its existence the waffle was worth no more than the equivalent of a penny or two. It contained no fresh ingredients, just treacle (readily available in any bakery), scraps of dough, crumbs and snippets from previous batches of waffles. The cheap confection became known as 'biscuits for the poor'.

Different flavours

In the 19th century there were some one hundred treacle waffle makers in Gouda and the product was exclusive to the city. Later, vendors began making and selling the confection at markets and feasts outside Gouda, and the treacle waffle became known all over the Netherlands.

By 1960 there were only seventeen treacle waffle manufacturers left in Gouda. Today that number has dwindled to four, each with their own secret recipe. Despite the waffle's relatively simple method of preparation there are many variations in flavour, and connoisseurs often have a preferred address for their supply.

Treacle waffles are popular. The Dutch eat about twenty a year, each. On the markets they are available in many different sizes, from mini to extra large. Treacle waffles are so delicious that the crumbs are always eaten too, as is every last drop of treacle.

Send for supplies

Every once in a while Dutch nationals living abroad find themselves missing their favourite Dutch treats such as *drop* and treacle waffles. In the past many a letter was written to family members back home pleading for supplies, but the digital highway has put an end to all that. A mere click of the mouse is all it takes to place an order with one of the numerous Dutch food shops on the internet.

In this way millions of treacle waffles have found their way overseas. With an enterprising spirit you could even order a waffle iron and set up your own market stall in waffle-less parts of the world. ∎

02 & 04 Production of treacle waffles at a market in Utrecht

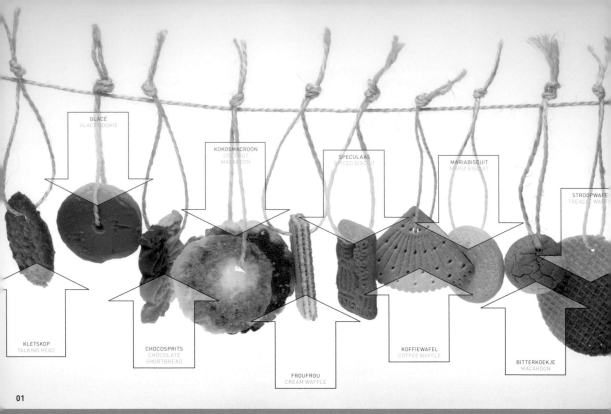

GLACÉ
GLACÉ COOKIE

KOKOSMACROON
COCONUT
MACAROON

SPECULAAS
SPICED BISCUIT

MARIABISCUIT
MARIA BISCUIT

STROOPWAFEL
TREACLE WAFFLE

KLETSKOP
TALKING HEAD

CHOCOSPRITS
CHOCOLATE
SHORTBREAD

FROUFROU
CREAM WAFFLE

KOFFIEWAFEL
COFFEE WAFFLE

BITTERKOEKJE
MACAROON

01

BISCUITS, CAKES & PASTRIES

the cookie Mecca

APART FROM TREACLE WAFFLES, THE DUTCH ARE FOND OF ABOUT EVERY SORT OF COOKIE, CAKE AND PASTRY IMAGINABLE. YET, AT THE SAME TIME THEY ARE KNOWN FOR THEIR FRUGALITY. ACCORDING TO A WIDESPREAD BELIEF, VISITORS WILL ONLY BE SERVED ONE BISCUIT WITH THEIR COFFEE.

02

03

04

05

Frugality is one of the most persistent clichés used to label the Dutch, who have been known to offer a single biscuit with the coffee and then close the biscuit tin quickly as if their entire savings were hidden inside. The Dutch are said to be tight-fisted and this seems to prove it.

In fact, economy is indeed a characteristic common to many Dutch people: they don't squander their money and are careful with their possessions. But hospitality is just as often attributed to the Dutch as frugality, if not more, and for every individual who thinks he is being generous serving a biscuit with the coffee at all, there are many more who leave the tin open on the table and invite their guests to help themselves. And they will probably personally set the example, being the greatest of cookie addicts themselves.

Huge assortment

The shelves laden with biscuits and sweets in Dutch supermarkets speak for themselves. The selection of biscuits alone covers numerous shelves, and will include *bitterkoekjes*, small, round, almond cookies; shortbread *spritsen*; cinnamon-flavoured *bastogne* biscuits; *bokkepootjes*, meringues dipped in chocolate; *krakelingen*, figure-of-eight cracknels; as well as biscuits that were once regional delicacies, such as *Weesper moppen*, almond-flavoured shortbreads; and *Arnhemse meisjes*, sugar-coated ovals of puff pastry. And these are but a handful from the overwhelming assortment available to the Dutch consumer.

The ins and outs of dunking

In the Netherlands eating biscuits is often accompanied by a rather strange ritual. One in three Dutch people habitually dip their biscuit into their tea, coffee or other hot drink before eating it, according to a survey carried out by biscuit manufacturer Verkade. This dunking is frowned upon by visiting foreigners. Do the Dutch have poor teeth?
The answer is no. They just like dunking their biscuit, especially if it's a plain biscuit, and have usually been taught to do so at a young age. Apparently seventy per cent of the dunkers started dunking before their 14th birthday and most of them have no qualms about dunking in company.
Verkade also discovered that there is a hidden motive for dunking a biscuit, one that dunkers themselves may not be aware of: dunking enhances the flavour of the biscuit. If you dip a biscuit into cold chocolate milk for eight seconds, its flavour becomes eleven times more intense. If you look at it like that, it remains a mystery why dunkers prefer to dunk in hot drinks.

Birthday cakes...

The assortment of cake and pastries is just as large as the selection of biscuits, and really comes into its element at birthdays. The host or hostess will welcome guests by offering them a cup of coffee and a large piece of cake as soon as they come in. Taking the coffee in one hand and the cake, wobbling

02 An employee of bakery De Groot in Den Bosch proudly presents a plate full of *Bosche bollen*, a delicious speciality of the town **03 & 04** *Tompouce* and the danger of eating it **05** The traditional game of *koekhappen* **06** Fruit flan bakers in Slenaken **07** Small strawberry pie, prepared according to traditional methods by the bakers of the De Bijenkorf department store **08** Wedding cake

06

07

08

09

Mmm...

10 Old-fashioned cookie tin from famous biscuit manufacturer Verkade

Verkade
BISCUITS

precariously on its plate, in the other, they are then faced with the rather awkward task of managing both under the friendly gaze of the rest of the guests. Luckily Dutch cakes are delicious almost by definition. Take the thick cream cakes, for example, such as the egg nog-flavoured 'snow star'; or the rich fruit flans like the famous *Limburg vlaaien*; or one of the many varieties with meringue. They are all guaranteed to turn any party into a success. Sometimes pastries are served instead of cake. All-time birthday favourites among young and old include the apple turnover, the *tompouce* (a cream slice covered in pink icing), hazelnut meringues, the *Bosche bol* (a huge round chocolate éclair), cheesecake and the fruit tartlet. Of course they're all laden with calories, but then it's not your birthday every day.

Utrecht shortbread

A delicious biscuit which is a speciality of the city of Utrecht.

Ingredients (for ten biscuits)

150 g butter	1 egg white
100 g raw white sugar	200 g flour
2 sachets of vanilla sugar	a pinch of salt

Preparation

Preheat oven to 175° C. Put the butter and the sugar into a bowl and mix until smooth. Add the vanilla sugar and salt and mix together well. Stir in the egg white and the sieved flour; continue stirring until the mixture is light and airy. Now grease a baking tray. Fill a piping bag with the mixture and, using a large serrated nozzle, squeeze it onto the baking tray in a wide zigzag. Place the tray at the bottom of the oven and bake the shortbread for fifteen to twenty minutes until light brown. Cut the shortbread into sizeable pieces and lift them out of the tray with a spatula. Allow to cool on an even surface.

...and games

No children's birthday party would be complete without cake or pastries, but unlike the adult gatherings, the party's success depends on a very different type of cake: *ontbijtkoek*, or breakfast cake, one of the plainest varieties available. This is the main ingredient in the traditional party game *koekhappen*, or 'bite-the-cake'. Participants are blindfolded, spun around, and then have to try and eat a slice of breakfast cake dangling from a string above them without using their hands. To make it even more difficult, the slices of cake are hung just out of reach, so the children have to stand on their tiptoes to get the last bites. The first one to finish wins the game, to the annoyance of the other little participants, who invariably start clamouring that their slices were just that bit higher than the winner's.

Get your skates on

Cakes are also closely linked with one of the Netherlands' most popular winter pastimes: ice-skating. As soon as the lakes and canals freeze over, the Dutch take to the ice *on masse*.
Traditionally, to fortify body and soul along the way, stalls set up along the route would sell *gevulde koeken* (large cake-like biscuits filled with almond paste), *jenever* (Dutch gin) and thick pea soup with sausage. Nowadays the Dutch gin has been replaced by hot chocolate and whipped cream, but the pea soup and *gevulde koeken* are as popular as ever. Indeed the selection of biscuits and cakes available at these stalls gets bigger each year.
Even with their skates on the Dutch have an incorrigibly sweet tooth. ■

12 Blueberry-meringue pie, prepared according to traditional methods by the bakers of the De Bijenkorf department store

festivals & holidays

On festivals and holidays, the Dutch like to dine copiously, but they don't care much for traditional meals and dishes. Customary delicacies, on the other hand, are very popular. And for Dutch children eating pancakes is always a feast.

01 A happy child with an Easter egg. Hiding painted eggs for the children is a popular Dutch Easter tradition

SAINT NICHOLAS

sweets for the sweet

'NEVER ACCEPT SWEETS FROM A STRANGER,' IMPLORE PARENTS. DUTCH PARENTS HOWEVER DO MAKE AN EXCEPTION ONCE A YEAR, WHEN A MAN WITH A WHITE BEARD TRAVELS THE LAND SCATTERING SWEETS ALL AROUND HIM. THIS IS ST. NICHOLAS, WHO PLAYS THE MAIN ROLE IN THE NETHERLANDS' MOST POPULAR FAMILY CELEBRATION.

Most Dutch people have forgotten all about their saints, but they still hold St. Nicholas (or *Sinterklaas* for short) in the highest regard, especially until they reach the age of about ten. *Sinterklaas* arrives in the Netherlands each year at the end of November, always accompanied by his Moorish helpers, the *Zwarte Pieten*, or 'Black Piets', and his trusty mare.

From that moment on, the entire country is consumed by *Sinterklaas* fever, which reaches a climax on December 5, or *pakjesavond*, the eve of the anniversary of the saint's death. On that evening, the Dutch give presents – lots of presents – to their friends and family. The children firmly believe that theirs don't come from their parents, but from the ever-generous saint.

Saintly behaviour

Special sweets play an important role in the traditional celebrations surrounding *Sinterklaas*. In the weeks before the 5th of December, the Dutch indulge in *speculaaspoppen*, spicy biscuits rather similar to gingerbread men, as well as *pepernoten*, spicy nut-like sweets; *taaitaai*, a rather chewy kind of gingerbread; pastries; marzipan figures and chocolate letters. And before they

go to bed, children, very seriously and very hopefully, sing *Sinterklaas* songs to encourage 'the *Sint*' to come and fill the shoe that they have left for him with all kinds of goodies.

On the evening of the 5th of December, sweets literally fly through Dutch living rooms. Throwing *pepernoten* is one of the many well-loved traditions that prevails at this time of year. It has its roots in the legends around St. Nicholas that have developed over the centuries.

In one story, Nicholas, who was bishop of Myra, in present-day Turkey, in around 300 AD, is said to have saved three sisters from a life of poverty and prostitution by throwing bags of money into their house. In earlier times, it was coins, not sweets that were thrown around on the 5th of December. Today, *pepernoten* and bags of chocolate coins do the job just as well.

The significance of *speculaas*

Speculaaspoppen, too, are inseparable from the *Sinterklaas* tradition. They stem from pre-Christian times, when it was traditional in north-western Europe to offer loaves of bread to Wodan, the Germanic god who rode his horse Sleipnir through the heavens on autumn nights. The bread was made on a board into which figures had been carved. When the bread, and later the *speculaas* figures, were taken off the board, they came out as a mirror image of the carved figures (*speculum* is Latin for 'mirror').

Speculaasjes

Ingredients
(for 12-15 *speculaasjes*)

400 g flour
2.5 tsp baking powder
1.5 tsp mixed spices (cinnamon, nutmeg, clove, ginger, cardamom, white pepper)
200 g butter
250 g brown sugar
75 g almond flakes
1 egg, pinch of salt

You will also need a *speculaas* mould.

Preparation

Combine the baking powder, mixed spices, salt and sifted flour. Add the sugar and butter. Knead to form a smooth dough and place in the fridge overnight to release the flavour of the spices. Preheat the oven to a medium heat, 170° C. Sprinkle the mould with flour. Knead the dough once more and press it into the mould. Trim off any excess. Turn the mould upside down and strike it so the figures fall out. Place on a greased baking sheet, sprinkle with almond flakes and brush with the lightly beaten egg. Don't forget to sprinkle the mould with flour before refilling it. Bake the *speculaasjes* for 20-25 minutes until brown. Turn them over during the last five minutes of baking.

Ancient *speculaas* moulds had figures such as the solar wheel, in honour of the Germanic festival of the solstice, and the heart, symbol of love. As the *Sinterklaas* tradition developed, *speculaaspoppen* took on a heart-warming significance. Giving a *speculaaspop* to someone meant that you were offering your hand in marriage.

Alongside *speculaaspoppen*, other sweets associated with *Sinterklaas* also connote love or marriage; fondant hearts for example, and the pastry letter filled with almond paste is part of this tradition too.

Pigging out

Another popular confection associated with *Sinterklaas*, also with Germanic roots, is the marzipan pig. The wild boar was a Germanic symbol of the hunt and a favourite animal for sacrifice. After animal sacrifices had been forbidden by the Church, people began to make animals from marzipan.

These days, the marzipan pig faces competition from a host of other figures, from fruit and *Sinterklaas* faces to toilets and mobile phones. St. Nicholas, it seems, moves with the times. But by far the most popular *Sinterklaas* confection has no connection at all with the pagan past: the chocolate letter. Each child receives at least one of these edible delights, traditionally the first letter of the child's first name. And while manufacturers

TRY ME →

Fondant (*Borstplaat*)

Ingredients

4 tbsp water, milk or cream
12 tbsp sugar
extract of vanilla
lemon
cocoa or raspberry
some cocoa powder or
instant coffee (optional)

Preparation

Mix the sugar with the water, milk or cream and bring slowly to the boil. Allow the mixture to boil for five minutes. It is ready when a drop placed in cold water turns hard. Remove the saucepan from the heat and stir in the extract. Pour the syrup onto a greased baking sheet and cut figures into it when it is almost hard. Allow the figures to harden completely, and then slide them from the baking sheet.

do their best to make each letter equally weighty, it's no surprise that some children, particularly those called Ingrid or Iris, pull a face when they see their friends named Michael or William opening their letters. Sometimes life just doesn't seem fair.∎

07 During the days before December 5, children place their shoe by the chimney, leaving a carrot or some hay in it for the saint's horse. According to tradition, the holy man rides over the rooftops on a grey horse, dropping gifts through the chimney in the shoes

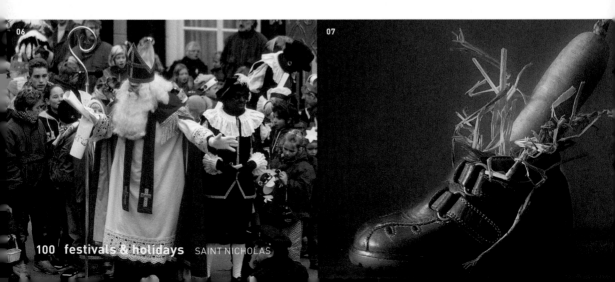

anything goes

MANY COUNTRIES SERVE TRADITIONAL MEALS ON FESTIVALS AND HOLIDAYS, BUT THE DUTCH TEND TO BE SOMEWHAT AVERSE TO SUCH DISHES. WHILE THEY PUT A LOT OF EFFORT INTO THEIR HOLIDAY DINNERS, THEY COOK WHATEVER TAKES THEIR FANCY. THEY DO HOWEVER ENJOY NUMEROUS CUSTOMARY DELICACIES.

XMAS, NEW YEAR & EASTER

01

TRY ME

Oliebollen

Ingredients

250 g flour	50 g currants
5 g salt	50 g raisins
5 g cinnamon	grated rind of half a lemon
2.5 dl milk (lukewarm)	25 g shredded candied peel
12 g yeast	(optional)
half an egg	half an apple,
a knob of butter	chopped (optional)
1 tbsp syrup	oil for frying

You will also need an ice-cream scoop and a skimmer.

Preparation

Mix together the flour, salt and cinnamon in a large mixing bowl. Make a well in the centre and break the egg into it. Dissolve the yeast in half of the milk and add to the flour mixture. Add a little more milk and stir to form a smooth batter. Leave to rest in a warm place until it froths. Melt the butter in a saucepan. Add the rest of the milk to the melted butter and then mix in the syrup. Now add this mixture to the batter and mix until smooth. Add the currants, sultanas and grated lemon peel. Cover the batter with a damp tea towel and let it rise to twice its size. Heat enough oil to completely immerse the *oliebollen*. Stir the candied peel and diced apple into the batter (if desired). Fill an ice-cream scoop with the batter and gently slide the batter into the oil. Test the temperature of the oil by first frying one *oliebol* until golden brown all over. Cut it in half. The *oliebol* should be done on the inside. Fry the remaining batter one scoop at a time, taking care that the *oliebollen* do not stick together. Let them drain on absorbent kitchen paper and serve sprinkled with icing sugar.

There aren't a lot of festivals in the Dutch calendar, and the most important (Christmas, New Year's Eve and Saint Nicholas – SEE PAGE 98) all fall in the month of December. Those visiting the Netherlands at the end of the year will find themselves knee-deep in chocolate letters, Christmas pastry rings, sweet Christmas breads, *oliebollen* (heavy doughnuts served to bring in the New Year) and apple fritters, all an integral part of the celebrations. But those expecting some kind of grand national dish as the highlight of this holiday month will be sorely disappointed.

Christmas biscuits and cakes

As Christmas approaches and Dutch people start making their plans for Christmas dinner, they invariably ask each other the same question: 'And, is the rabbit getting fat?' That might lead the listener to assume that rabbit is a typical Christmas dish, but there is too much variation in the Christmas menu to speak of any one traditional meal.

Finding a Dutch equivalent to the English stuffed turkey requires digging deep into the national culinary archives. Until the 1940s, goose was the quintessential Christmas dish. But goose, fat or not, became too expensive for many and a lot of Dutch families chose chicken instead.

However, towards the end of the 20th century, chicken was considered too 'common' for a holiday dinner and since then the Dutch have let their culinary wiles take them where they will. Many people 'do something' with chicken or game, while others do something else with fish, a roulade or a foreign dish.

What do unite the nation's kitchens at Christmas however are the traditional cakes and biscuits: the *kerstkrans*, a pastry ring filled with almond paste; *kerstkransjes*, biscuit rings sprinkled with sugar and almond flakes; and the Christmas *stol*, a sweet bread filled with currants, sultanas, candied peel and almond paste. A few months later, at Easter, the same delicacies appear once more, but this time re-christened as Easter pastry rings, Easter bread and Easter biscuits.

New Year treats

As with Christmas, New Year's Eve boasts no traditional menu, but does have its own sweet treats: *oliebollen* (literally 'oil balls'), deep-fried, ball-shaped doughnuts, and *appelflappen* or apple fritters, battered and fried apple rings. Both are served on New Year's Eve, liberally sprinkled with icing sugar.

Some regions in the Netherlands still retain their own traditional New Year specialities. In the northern province of Drenthe, people make *spekken-dikken*, thin bacon rashers wrapped in thick waffles that are supposed to bring good luck. Traditionally, one of the bacon rashers is replaced with a piece of cloth. The unfortunate recipient of this *spekkendik* will find he has bitten off more than he can chew. In the province of North Holland, a lightly sweetened bread called *duivekater* is served on New Year's Day. It reappears at Easter and Whitsun.■

02 A Christmas *stol* **03** New Year's Eve celebration **04** An original *krentenwegge*, a traditional kingsize currant bread (see page 9) **05** Chocolate Easter bunny **06 & 07** Easter delicacies at a shop in Culemborg **09** A cool Easter chick **11** A *boterlammetje*

05

01

Eggs and *boterlammetjes*

When it comes to food, Easter is all about eggs, age-old symbols of fertility that live on in the Easter tradition. Painted, they are hidden for children to find; boiled, they are enjoyed as part of the Easter breakfast. Small chocolate eggs are eaten with coffee or tea throughout the Easter period and a common gift for children is an Easter bunny (in the Netherlands it's actually a hare), carrying a basket of those same eggs on his back.

Another Easter tradition that has stood the test of time is the *boterlammetje* or butter lamb. In the 17th century, farmers in south-western Holland fashioned moulds made from beechwood in the shape of lambs. These they used for grass-butter, which was made from the first milk that cows produced once they had returned to the pastures in spring. The little butter lambs were then presented to the lord of the manor. These days, butter lambs still appear at the breakfast table on Easter Sunday. Easter dinner is similar to that served at Christmas in that a lot of time and effort is put into its preparation, but it is not characterized by any one particular dish. Again, the Dutch follow their current whim. Perhaps the reason for this is that the Dutch enjoy their food so much that they refuse to be bound by national traditions – with the exception of those cakes and biscuits.

06

07

08

09

11

the tastiest of treats

ASK A DUTCH CHILD WHAT HIS FAVOURITE FOOD IS AND TEN TO ONE HE WILL SHOUT: 'PANCAKES!' THIS TYPICAL DUTCH FOOD USED TO BE EATEN AS A HEARTY BREAKFAST BY THE DUTCH PEASANTRY. TODAY, THE DUTCH SEE IT MORE AS A CHILDREN'S TREAT, ALONGSIDE ITS MINIATURE BROTHER, THE *POFFERTJE*.

01

APPLE

SYRUP

SUGAR

CHERRIES

CHEESE

MUSHROOMS

BACON

04 Eating pancakes at the famous pancake house De Vuursche Boer in Lage Vuursche **05** The *poffertjes* at equally famous Victor Consael in Utrecht are a treat, too

The pancakes served in the famous pancake houses of Lage Vuursche and Bunnik are almost as big as old-fashioned wagon wheels. Just one will see you through the whole day.

Put a plate of medium-sized pancakes in front of a Dutch child and you can be sure of some peace and quiet for a while. Even the faddiest young eater has been known to magically develop a huge appetite and blissfully eat his way through a huge number of pancakes.

The first pancake will be sprinkled with icing sugar, the second with a thick layer of syrup, the next with icing sugar again and so on until his pancake craving has been fully satisfied. Adults too are partial to a pancake from time to time, often preparing a more savoury version for themselves by adding slices of apple or bacon.

As big as wagon wheels

Making pancakes at home is a treat for the kids, but an even bigger treat is going to a pancake house, a restaurant that specialises in pancakes. There are pancake houses all over the Netherlands, but they tend to be less popular in the northern provinces of Groningen, Friesland and Overijssel than in the rest of the country.

The Netherlands' most celebrated pancake houses are to be found in Lage Vuursche and Bunnik. The pancakes served here, in idyllic surroundings, are almost as big as old-fashioned wagon wheels. Just one will see you through the whole day.

Pancake-lovers in the province of Zeeland can even enjoy their favourite food aboard a ship. A round trip on a boat through the Oosterschelde National Park leaves from the former island of Neeltje Jans, which now forms part of the spectacular Storm Surge Barrier in the Oosterschelde, a popular tourist attraction. The crew serves up pancakes throughout the trip.

Prehistoric pancakes

Pancakes date back to pre-history. Primitive people used a stone to grind grain, rye, wheat, millet or buckwheat into flour that was then mixed with water. The batter was baked on hot stones to form a thin kind of bread. It wasn't long before they discovered that the mixture tasted better when they added eggs. In the 19th century pancakes formed part of the peasant's three 'breakfasts'. These three morning meals were extremely nourishing. The day started with a few slices of bread, followed a few hours later by porridge and pancakes fried in bacon fat, and then by a third meal of potatoes. The Dutch rural population continued eating porridge and pancakes for breakfast well into the 20th century.
Variations on the pancake can be found the world over, from the thin French *crêpe* to the Indian *dosa*, or rice pancake. The Dutch pancake is known for its substance and is generally served with icing sugar,

syrup, apple slices, bacon or cheese, or a combination of these: apple and bacon, apple and raisins or bacon and cheese. Even a plain Dutch pancake is an indulgence it's hard to say 'no' to.

The pancake is linked with Dutch culture in another way, too. The Dutch countryside itself is described as being 'as flat as a pancake' in one popular saying.

Windy little friars

Pancake batter is also used to make *poffertjes*: small, thick pancakes, about two cm in diameter, served by the plateful with butter and powdered sugar. This sweet dish is more of a delicacy than a meal and its origins are, rather surprisingly, religious.

Poffertjes were originally made to be served as a form of host in a Dutch abbey. During the French revolution the monks, faced with a shortage of wheat flour, started making the batter with buckwheat flour instead, and the result was a thicker and even tastier host.

As in many monasteries at the time, the friars traded goods with market sellers and merchants, and when they tasted this new type of host at communion they immediately saw its commercial potential. They bought the recipe from its creators and ordered a blacksmith to make a furnace with two hundred small hollows in the top plate, on which they began making what they dubbed 'little friars'. The noise of air escaping from the 'little friars' when they were done however, soon had people calling them *poffertjes*.

Family recipes

The production of *poffertjes* fell into the hands of six Dutch families, whose names are still familiar with lovers of Dutch confectionary today. Over the years these families improved the flavour by adding ingredients of their own. The ensuing new recipes where passed down the generations in strict secrecy. These families' descendants still make *poffertjes* according to their specific family recipe today, selling the miniature pancakes from attractive stalls on markets and squares, just like their ancestors did before them. Children passing by find it hard to resist the seductive sweet smell of *poffertjes*, often needing gentle coercion from their parents to move on. ∎

06

TRY ME

Bacon pancakes

Ingredients (serves 6)

2 eggs
1 kg wheat or buckwheat flour
0.5 l milk
0.5 l lukewarm water
1 pinch of salt
24 rashers of (streaky) bacon
butter

Preparation

Beat the eggs and pour into a bowl with the flour and half of the milk. Blend until smooth. Stir in the rest of the milk, the water and the salt. Melt a knob of butter in a frying pan. Ladle some batter into the frying pan and allow it to spread out evenly. Lay four rashers of (streaky) bacon on top of the batter and bake the pancake until light brown on both sides. Add extra flavour with syrup or sugar.

storante Pizzeria
FUSTO D'ORO

KFC

RIEKS SPECIALITEITEN RESTAURANT
MYKONOS

NDISCH RESTA
SELAMAT MA

TOPKAPI
RESTAURANT

ABRIKOS
Mediterraans & Tapas
RESTAURANT

Oriëntaalse Gered

PIAZZA
D'Oro

Grieks
Ecthuis

L'ARTISTA

TAVERN.

HINESE K

foreign delight

Dos Locos
TAPAS & ZO

PASSAGE TO INDIA
INDIAN-TANDOORI
RESTAURANT

KING
ARTHUR
Drinks
& More

TURKS RESTAURAN

In the last fifty years Dutch society has become multi-cultural, and as a result the Dutch culinary landscape has been enriched by countless foreign influences. Gastronomic treats from countries like Indonesia, China, Turkey, Surinam, Italy and Morocco can be enjoyed in eateries all over the country.

01

treats from the Emerald Belt

FROM ALL FOREIGN INFLUENCES ON THE DUTCH EATING HABITS, THOSE FROM THE FORMER DUTCH EAST INDIES ARE THE MOST ESTABLISHED. QUITE A FEW DISHES FROM THE 'EMERALD BELT', AS PRESENT-DAY INDONESIA IS STILL POETICALLY CALLED, ARE COMPLETELY ASSIMILATED INTO DUTCH COOKING.

02

foreign delight · INDO-FOOD

03   04   05

01 & 02 Drawings depicting daily life in the Dutch East Indies
03 & 04 Indonesian *rijsttafel*, served on banana leafs at the Indonesian restaurant Sampurna in Amsterdam **05** Foreign delights in the supermarket

Until its formal independence in 1949, Indonesia was subject to strong Dutch influence for some 350 years, and was a Dutch colony for about the last 150 years of that period. Many Dutch people living in the Dutch East Indies enjoyed the exotic food, aside from periodic bouts of nostalgia for potatoes and cheese. They may have had to learn not to mash the various foods together, but this habit was quickly unlearned.

Rijsttafel

Rice plays a main part in Indonesian cuisine. Just as in modern Indonesia, rice was usually prepared in the morning in the Indies, together with vegetable, meat or fish dishes, so that there would be food for the entire family all day long
The Dutch were used to eating only one hot meal a day, but in the Indies they switched to two rice-based meals a day. Initially they found this rather heavy, as the side dishes almost all contained large quantities of *bumbu bumbu*, fresh spices such as ginger and turmeric, coriander seed and lemongrass. These dishes were also prepared with generous helpings of onions and garlic, flavours that occurred in Dutch cooking only in modest amounts. Popular among the Dutch was the *rijsttafel* (literally 'rice table'), consisting of a wide range of dishes. Contrary to popular belief, however, the *rijsttafel* is not an authentic Indonesian meal. Traditionally, native Indonesians ate simple meals consisting of boiled white rice and one or two spiced dishes. Multiple dishes were prepared only for holidays and memorials.
Among the Dutch, the festive meal consisting of rice, two vegetable dishes, meat, fish and chicken, proved more popular than its more modest variant. With the expertise of the *kokki*, an Indonesian female cook, Chinese and Malay dishes began to appear

> **Many Dutch people living in the Dutch East Indies enjoyed the exotic food, aside from periodic bouts of nostalgia for potatoes and cheese.**

on the table, such as *lumpia* (fried pancakes filled with meat and vegetables) and *sateh* (grilled meat on skewers), alongside Indonesian food. This made visible the ethnic diversity of the 'Emerald Belt', as the Indies were poetically called.

Secrets of tropical cuisine

The home front, which had initially been limited to reading about culinary adventures overseas, was introduced to Indonesian cuisine in the early 20th century. The prestigious Bijenkorf department store in Rotterdam introduced the Dutch to secrets of

tropical cuisine through demonstrations of Indonesian dishes. This resulted in some surprise regarding matters such as how both cultures ate rice. Rice was once condescendingly considered 'chicken feed' in the Netherlands and traditionally used mostly in the preparation of rice pudding, a sticky dessert eaten with brown sugar and a hefty lump of butter. When the Dutch cooked rice, they added lemon juice to the water to make the rice dry and extra white. This sent shivers down the spines of Indonesians who heard about these practices. They cooked their rice in plain water until dry. In the meantime they would peel and chop onions and garlic, crushing them together with all sorts of spices with a mortar and pestle until a savoury mixture was achieved. This was first fried in oil and then finely chopped vegetables or cubes of meat were added.

Tokos and pasar malams

Although many saw the preparation of Indonesian food as labour-intensive because of the spices required, the *rijsttafel* quickly gained a foothold on the Dutch menu. Nowadays, *sateh*, *krupuk* (wafer-thin fried shrimp crackers) and *sambal* (a spicy sauce made from red peppers and peanuts) are completely assimilated into Dutch cooking. Those looking to cook their own Indonesian food can find ingredients at the many *tokos*, or Indonesian spice shops. Many Dutch people regularly visit Indonesian restaurants or enjoy Indonesian meals at frequent *pasar malams*, or covered Indonesian markets. Even snack bars serve Indonesian treats. The huge popularity of *sateh*, *bami* (noodles) and *nasi* means

these foods are ubiquitous, but disguised as greasy *sateh* croquettes, *bami* balls and *nasi* encased in breading and deep-fried, these hardly qualify as exotic treats anymore.

The Dutch who returned from the Indies developed their own cuisine in the meantime. Potatoes, Brussels sprouts and cheese are liberally doused with *sambal*, and dishes such as potatoes with *ayam semur* (braised chicken) and rice with shredded beef are served. ■

TRY ME →

Nasi goreng Belanda

Nasi goreng was originally made from leftover white rice. The ham and peas give it a Dutch touch.

Ingredients (serves 4)

400 g white rice	2 thick slices of ham
1 large onion	1 leek
2 cloves of garlic	1 tin of peas
1 tsp *terasi* (shrimp paste)	3 eggs
salt	oil
pepper	1 tsp *sambal ulek* (optional)

Preparation

Cook the white rice in a pot with plenty of water until it is just about done and allow it to cool down uncovered. Chop the onion, press the garlic cloves until fine and crumble the *terasi*. Heat the oil in a heavy-bottomed pan and fry the onion and garlic with salt until fragrant. Add the *terasi*. Stir well to prevent sticking. Now add the rice a little at a time and continue to stir so that the ingredients do not stay at the bottom. Cut the ham into small cubes and the leek into thin rounds and add them together with the peas. In a separate bowl, beat the eggs lightly and cook an omelette, cutting it into thin strips. Add the strips to the *nasi*. Season with pepper, salt and *sambal ulek* (if desired).

popular Asian fusion cuisine

THE INTRODUCTION IN THE 1950s OF CHINESE-INDONESIAN RESTAURANTS, WHICH CAN NOW BE FOUND ALL OVER THE COUNTRY, DRAMATICALLY CHANGED THE DUTCH GASTRONOMIC LANDSCAPE. THE DUTCH CHANGED FROM CULINARY INTROVERTS WHO SELDOM ATE OUTSIDE THE HOME INTO ADVENTURERS WITH AN UNPARALLELED INTEREST IN EXOTIC FOOD.

01

02 © SFA

03

05

04

06

'Going to the Chinese' and 'getting a Chinese' are expressions all Dutch people understand. They don't mean they're about to travel to China or adopt a Chinese child. Instead, they're talking about going to a Chinese restaurant, or usually a Chinese-Indonesian one, or picking up a meal. These Asian restaurants are so familiar that many Dutch consider them almost Dutch. Only a few are aware of their fascinating history, closely linked to the maritime and colonial past, that introduced the Dutch to 'exotic' food.

Chinese eateries

The first Chinese in the Netherlands arrived in 1890, working in merchant shipping and living in boarding houses in the Katendrecht area of Rotterdam and the Nieuwmarkt area in Amsterdam. The economic recession of the 1930s and the Second World War cost many of them their jobs. Some returned to China, those who remained attempted to survive by selling peanut cakes in the streets.

The two Chinese neighbourhoods saw the emergence of eateries – really little more than living rooms with some tables and chairs – serving authentic Chinese food. The portions were remarkably large and cheap, and the first customers were, not surprisingly, people who had little money: Chinese students from the Dutch East Indies (now Indonesia), indigenous Chinese and itinerant artists. Later, these eateries were also popular among Dutch people who had lived in the Indies and sailors who were used to eating *nasi* (white rice) in the East. Dutch civilians were hesitant to set foot in these establishments until they discovered that Dutch was spoken and beer was served there.

Chinese becomes Chinese-Indonesian

The creation of an independent Indonesia in 1949 led to the arrival of large numbers of Indonesian Dutch citizens and returning Dutch civilians and military personnel from the former colony. Chinese restaurateurs cleverly exploited this by adding to their typical Chinese dishes such as *lumpia* (fried pancakes filled with meat and vegetables) and *babi panggang* (grilled pork) such things as *nasi goreng* (fried rice), *gado-gado* (cooked vegetables in peanut sauce), *krupuk* (wafer-thin shrimp crackers) and *sateh* (grilled meat on a skewer). They also increasingly hired Indonesian chefs in addition to Chinese ones. Indonesian food at Chinese restaurants became popular, with more and more Chinese eateries advertising themselves as Chinese-Indonesian restaurants. In the early 1960s, in addition to twenty Chinese eateries in Amsterdam and Rotterdam, the Netherlands already had more than two hundred Chinese-Indonesian restaurants. Unchanging low prices and huge portions created a national addiction to Chinese food.

Differences

Chinese and Indonesian dishes go together very well, but there are nonetheless major differences between the two cuisines. Chinese food makes frequent use of pork, which is seldom eaten in Indonesia, a mostly Muslim country. Pungent spices such as *lombok* (cayenne pepper) and flavourings such as *terasi* (made from shrimp) and *sambal* (red pepper paste) are essential to Indonesian cooking, while the Chinese prefer garlic, sesame seeds, dried mushrooms, ginger and sweet-and-sour sauces. Rice is always a main ingredient in Indonesian food, while Chinese cooking also includes noodle dishes.

There are also major differences in how dishes are prepared. Traditionally, Chinese dishes are stir-fried, steamed or grilled in an oven or over an open flame, to retain the original flavour of the ingredients. Indonesian chefs, on the other hand, change the flavour of the products by preparing them with herbs and spice mixes.

Culinary adventurer

The arrival of Chinese-Indonesian restaurants drastically altered Dutch food culture. Whereas people ate exclusively Dutch food, at home, they now enjoy exotic meals in restaurants and their experiences with Chinese-Indonesian cuisine have prepared them for a new role as culinary adventurers. Research shows that Dutch people have more exotic appetites when it comes to restaurant food than any other nationality – something that benefits the many thousands of international restaurants in the Netherlands. ∎

02 Chinese selling peanuts in Amsterdam in the early 1930s

> The Chinese-Indonesian restaurants are so familiar that many Dutch consider them almost Dutch.

TRY ME ➡

Foo Yong Hai

A typical Chinese dish consisting of an omelette filled with vegetables.

Ingredients (serves 4)

For the omelette
6 eggs
1 small leek
pepper
salt
For the filling
onion
garlic
350 g mixed vegetables
small tin of bamboo shoots
150 g beansprouts
For the sauce
2 dl chicken stock
4 tbsp tomato ketchup
1 tbsp brown sugar
2 tbsp *kecap manis* (sweet soy sauce)
1 tbsp powdered ginger
1.5 tsp cornflour

Preparation

Filling: Peel and chop the onion. Drain bamboo shoots. Heat oil in a wok, fry onion quickly and press the garlic into it. Sprinkle with salt and pepper. Stir-fry the mixed vegetables. Just before the vegetables are cooked, add the bamboo shoots and beansprouts. Stir until everything is cooked but still firm.
Omelette: Chop the white part of the leek. Beat the eggs lightly and mix in the leek, pepper and salt. Cook the omelette, making sure it is not too thin.
Sauce: Bring the chicken stock to a boil, add tomato ketchup, sugar, soy sauce and powdered ginger and cook the mixture over a low heat for two to three minutes, stirring continually. Mix the cornflour with two tablespoons of cold water, stir the mixture into the sauce and bring everything briefly to a boil.
Cover half of the omelette with the filling, fold the other half over it and pour the sauce over. Serve with boiled white rice and *krupuk*.

roti, kebabs & tajine

IN ADDITION TO INDONESIAN AND CHINESE CUISINE, MORE EXOTIC CULINARY TRADITIONS HAVE GAINED A FOOTHOLD IN THE NETHERLANDS. PEOPLE ARRIVING FROM COUNTRIES LIKE SURINAM, ITALY, TURKEY AND MOROCCO BROUGHT THEIR OWN FOOD CUSTOMS. TODAY THESE ARE AN INTEGRAL PART OF THE DUTCH CULINARY LANDSCAPE.

MULTI-CULTURAL, MULTI-CULINARY

As early as the 17th century, the Dutch were introduced to exotic products through the Dutch East India Company, the world's first multinational. This era also saw the first culinary cross-pollination in the form of such things as *nagelkaas*, a tasty alliance of Dutch farm cheese and cloves, and porridge made with milk and rice. But it was the introduction of the Chinese-Indonesian restaurant [SEE PAGE 113] which really made the Dutch familiar with 'exotic' cuisines and made them hunger for more.

A love of foreign food

Today, the Dutch are open to foreign culinary influences as no other nation. When they eat out, they love to try the newest exotic restaurant in town, and foreign specialities are welcome at home too. They like to experiment a bit with food from home and abroad, whether it involves spices, *feta* cheese, pizza bases or *couscous*.

Not that the Dutch are always experimenting. And why would they, with a pizzeria, a tapas bar, a Moroccan bakery, a Turkish takeaway and a Surinamese *roti* shop in the area, providing delicious ready-to-eat dishes? All that's needed is a good bike and a few euro and the food will still be hot when you get home, if you pedal hard enough.

Surinamese *roti*

Foreign influences are now an integral part of Dutch eating habits, but there has also been a Dutch influence on other cuisines. Spicy dishes gained milder variants and Italian restaurants offer pizzas that are not to be found in Italy.

The best example involves Dutch brown beans in the leading role, which have become the pride of the cuisine of the former Dutch colony Surinam. Surinam's national dish is 'BB and R', or brown beans and rice. The Dutch are not particularly fond of this culinary blend. They prefer a Surinamese *roti*, a folded pancake of meat, black-eyed peas and potatoes, also available in a delicious vegetarian version.

Pizza and *kebabs*

Italian food has traditionally been popular in the Netherlands. When they don't feel like cooking, the Dutch often bring home a pizza or pasta dinner, adding a salad made of vegetables from their own

The Dutch like to experiment with food from abroad, whether it involves spices, *feta* or *couscous*.

01 Different kinds of olives, for sale at the Olijven Plaza Nabil in Utrecht **02** Dishes from different cultures are served at the Hotel Bazar in Rotterdam **03** Surinamese restaurant Patoe in Culemborg **04** *Baklava*, a delicious Turkish dessert

fridge. Indifferent to the fact that in Italy pizza is really a snack and pasta is the second starter, the Dutch serve both as main courses.

Pizzas are also a popular part of Turkish food in the Netherlands, but the best-known Turkish dish is *shish kebab*, or grilled meat on skewers. Also popular is *döner kebab*, where the meat is served on bread and complemented by crunchy Dutch lettuce. Cognoscenti consider this a weak derivative of what the rich Turkish cuisine truly has to offer. The Turkish restaurant *Ana's Kusin* in Utrecht, for example, features food authentically prepared by Turkish mothers (*ana* means 'mother' in Turkish). A selection of *meze* (various hot and cold starters), *dolma* (stuffed vine leaves), *köfte* (meat), salads and honey-laden desserts such as *baklava* and *sutlac* means a lesson in culinary delight for the Dutch, who increasingly appreciate such things.

Couscous and tajine

Another famous Mediterranean cuisine, Moroccan, makes much use of *couscous*, or millet, a product that is as important to Moroccans as potatoes are to the Dutch. Vegetable and meat dishes are always served with *couscous*, but despite the similar roles of *couscous* and spuds, the Dutch prefer *tajine*, a stew of fish, meat or chicken with vegetables, prepared in the earthenware vessel of the same name. If any of the Moroccan bread that is always served with hot meals should remain, it will be topped with a few slices of ultra-Dutch cheese for breakfast the next day.■

Surinamese *roti*

A pancake with a savoury filling. The pancake (*roti*) is available in ready-to-use form at *tokos* and larger supermarkets.

Ingredients (serves 4)

For the filling
1 package of frozen green beans
4 small chicken filets
700 g pre-cooked potatoes or 8 medium potatoes
4 large cloves of garlic
2 medium onions
4 heaping tbsp *masala* spices
salt & pepper
herbs for chicken
sunflower oil

Preparation

Cut the chicken fillets into pieces and rub with salt and *masala*. Chop the onions and peel the garlic. Cut the peeled potatoes into quarters. Heat the oil in a large pan and fry the garlic and onion. Add the chicken and fry until light brown. Now add the uncooked potatoes together with three cups of water. Add the frozen green beans so that the mixture begins to cook. Simmer everything until the potatoes are done and the beans are soft. Add herbs, salt and pepper to taste. If the mixture dries out, add water immediately. Fill a *roti* halfway with the mixture. Fold the pancake in half and warm it up in a microwave for 1.5-2 minutes. Eat the *roti* with your hands, tearing off a piece of pancake at a time and using it to pick some of the filling.

07 Culinary cross-pollination from the beginning: *nagelkaas*, a tasty alliance of Dutch cheese and cloves from Indonesia **08** Iran-born Faranak proudly presents a home-made traditional meal. She lives in the Netherlands since 1995

07

08

fast food

Fast food is quick and easy, and whole generations seem to grow up in snack bars and automats. Older generations grumble that today's youth is lazy, and the Dutch government is considering a 'snack tax' to discourage consumption of fattening fare.

TRY ME →

Dutch meat croquette

Ingredients (for eight croquettes)

600 g cooked chicken or beef	pepper
1 finely diced onion	mace
60 g butter	ground nutmeg
60 g flour	flour
0.5 l bouillon	2-3 loosely beaten eggs
salt	breadcrumbs

Preparation

Cut or chop the meat very fine. Melt the butter in a saucepan and sauté the onion until translucent. Add the flour, bouillon, salt, pepper, mace and nutmeg and stir to make a roux; then add the meat. Allow the ragout to cool completely, then refrigerate until thoroughly cold. Shape into sausages, about ten cm long, and not too thick or they will need too much frying time. Take three deep plates, flouring one of them, putting beaten eggs in a second and breadcrumbs in the third. Now coat each croquette in flour, beaten egg and breadcrumbs – in that order – covering them liberally so that they don't split open during frying. Return them to the fridge for half an hour. Heat the frying oil and fry the croquettes until golden brown; place them on absorbent kitchen paper when done. Serve the croquettes with mustard.

FAST FOOD

snack till you crack

JUST AS WITH OTHER WESTERN COUNTRIES, FAST FOOD HAS THE NETHERLANDS IN SOMETHING OF A STRANGLEHOLD, POPULAR AS BOTH A QUICK SNACK BETWEEN MEALS AND AS A MEAL IN ITSELF. AND WITH LOTS OF SNACK BARS AROUND, YOU DON'T NEED YOUR OWN DEEP FRYER TO ENJOY THE TYPICALLY DUTCH CROQUETTE AND 'WAR FRIES'.

Snack bars are enjoying an unprecedented popularity in the Netherlands. With their long opening hours (often from noon until midnight), these greasy eateries are the perfect place to enjoy a savoury snack in the middle of the afternoon or late at night.

They are especially busy, however, in the early evening, when most Dutch people look forward to their one and only hot meal of the day. Customers crowd around the counter, shouting out orders as long as your arm. Snack bars vary from shabby hang-outs to smart, spotless cafés, and a significant number of them are run by Chinese, Vietnamese and Egyptians.

Make mine with mayo

The most popular snack by far is French fries, served either in a paper cone or plastic dish. Dutch fries are thicker than their slim French counterpart, but not as fat as the Belgian variety.
To the amazement of many foreigners, the Dutch usually eat their French fries with mayonnaise. In

To the amazement of many foreigners, the Dutch usually eat their French fries with mayonnaise.

a comical dialogue in the film *Pulp Fiction*, the main character, played by John Travolta, expresses his astonishment at *patat met*, or 'fries with'. With what? Well, usually with mayo, but tomato ketchup, spicy, tomato-flavoured curry sauce and peanut sauce are all common alternatives. *Patat speciaal* (fries with mayonnaise, ketchup and finely chopped onion) is also popular. One thoroughly Dutch speciality worthy of mention is *patatje oorlog* (literally 'war fries'), where the fries are generously covered with mayonnaise and peanut sauce and often supplemented with tomato ketchup and onions.

Patat-generation

For the older generations who grew up on more nourishing food, French fries are a poor alternative for 'real food'. They might fill your stomach, but have not much nutritional value or character. Their appeal lies in the fact that they are quick and easy. Referring to the general laziness of today's youth, former trainer Leo Beenhakker of Amsterdam's

03

football club Ajax called the team's junior players 'members of the *patat*-generation'. This pejorative won him as many fans as his successful stints as coach of such famous clubs as Ajax, Feyenoord and Real Madrid.

The *patat*-generation actually seems to appreciate its derogatory title. Its members enjoy their *fricadel*, *sitosticks*, and *lihanboutjes* – all unique to the Netherlands – with fervour. For the uninitiated, such names can hold out an almost mystic appeal, but aficionados know exactly what they will get when they order a *fricadel* (a hard, thin sausage), a *sitostick* (lean meat and onion rings) or a *lihanboutje* (deep-fried mince on a stick).

King croquette

But it's the *krokct*, a sausage-shaped snack, fried in breadcrumbs and filled with ragout, that is by far the most popular. It even comes in vegetarian and shrimp varieties.

The king of all croquettes is the Kwekkeboom croquette, or simply 'the Kwek'. It was invented by an Amsterdam pastry chef, Kwekkeboom, who produced a refined beef croquette at a time when other croquettes were made only with chicken or pork. The first bite is enough to convince any snacker that the recipe was put together with great care and attention, and they will usually only make do with an 'ordinary' croquette after tasting a Kwekkeboom croquette if there is really no option.

The croquette holds the number-one position in the Dutch snack top ten, closely followed by the *fricadel*. Next comes the *bamischijf*, a deep-fried cake of pressed noodles; the *nasibal*, a deep-fried ball of pressed rice; the *kaassoufflé*, melted cheese in a pillow of dough; *kipkorn*, a chicken creation on a stick; hamburgers; meatballs; *mexicano*, a spicy, rectangular *fricadel*; and the *lumpia*, or spring roll.

Don't tax my snacks!

In spite of the gusto with which the snack-happy *patat*-generation relishes its favourite food, its days of guilt-free enjoyment appear short-lived. Due

03 Enjoying fast food at the cafetaria Van Gogh in Nuenen, a village where the famous painter Vincent van Gogh once lived and worked **05** *Patat met*, or fries with mayonnaise **07** 'War fries'

to the alarming rise in obesity in the Netherlands, the government is planning to introduce measures to discourage consumption of fast food. Nearly a third of Dutch people are too heavy. One in seven children is overweight. Such statistics are not due to a drop in the quality of Dutch food – it has never been higher – but to the fact that Dutch people are eating too much in general and too much fatty food in particular. They also turn their noses up at physical exercise, the best way to shed those extra pounds. To counter this weighty problem, the Dutch government is considering the introduction of heavy measures – a so-called 'snack tax'. The idea is to hit the thrifty Dutch where they feel it most: in their wallets. It remains to be seen whether their natural sense of economy will make the Dutch strong enough to resist the urge to dive into the local snack bar when they smell those French fries. ■

slow
food

In modern times,
people who love to
cook sumptuously
have become
something of an
endangered species,
as are quite a few
labour-intensive
traditional dishes.
The Slow Food
movement promotes
'endangered' regional
specialities and the
proper way to prepare
them – with patience
and a smile.

01 Farmer between willow trees in Haastrecht

relaxing in the kitchen

THE RISE OF FAST FOOD AND CONVENIENCE FOODS HAS PUSHED THE CHARM OF COOKING TO THE BACKGROUND, WITH TRADITIONAL REGIONAL DISHES SUFFERING MOST. RECENTLY A MOVEMENT EMERGED THAT COUNTERACTS THIS TREND, AND OLD GASTRONOMIC VALUES ARE BEING REDISCOVERED UNDER THE 'SLOW FOOD' BANNER.

The Dutch Slow Food Foundation has compiled a list of 'endangered' regional products, including Gouda and Leiden farm cheese, Texel sheep cheese, Maastricht veal pie and Oosterschelde crab.

TRY ME →

Vijfschaft

An authentic Utrecht lunch from bygone times.

Ingredients (serves 4)

250 g brown beans	200 g sliced bacon
1 tsp salt	1 smoked sausage
250 g carrots	potato flour
2 onions	25 g butter
750 g potatoes	salt
2 tart apples	fresh ground pepper

Preparation

Soak the brown beans in a pan of water for 24 hours, then bring them to a boil in the same water with salt and cook them gently on a low heat for thirty minutes. Peel and dice the carrot. Clean the onions and cut them into rings. Peel and quarter the potatoes. Peel the apples, remove the cores and cut them into sections. Add the carrots, onions and potatoes to the beans, make sure everything is just covered by the water and bring to a boil. Let simmer for forty minutes on a low heat and add the apple in the last ten minutes. Meanwhile, steep the smoked sausage in hot water (not boiling) for fifteen minutes. Slowly fry the bacon in a pan until crisp. Drain the water into a pan and mix with potato flour to make a sauce. Stir in the butter and season to taste with salt and pepper. Place the *vijfschaft* in a pre-heated dish, pour the potato flour sauce over it and cover with slices of smoked sausage and crisp bacon.

02

Prepared products and meals are convenient but they also have a downside. Fewer and fewer people are taking the time to prepare or linger over a meal. Authentic regional dishes in particular are at risk of being forgotten, all the more because of the limited seasonal availability of the basic ingredients. Moreover, preparing them takes patience, time and planning, all of which are scarce these days.

This is how countless typical regional products lost ground, such as Limburg syrup, Amsterdam ox sausage, the Chaam hen and the Schellinkhout apple. To the delight of those who love diverse cuisine, the decline of gastronomic traditions resulted in a movement in the opposite direction.

Culinary renaissance

An initiative was started in Italy to maintain 'endangered' seasonal regional products and authentic methods of preparing regional specialities, including farm cheeses, traditional meats, breads, old types of fruit and vegetables, rare livestock breeds and unusual fish and shellfish. With a nod to the fast food phenomenon, this broad re-evaluation of regional dishes and the idea of learning to enjoy food again are known as 'slow food'.
The idea has received attention in the Netherlands as well. The Dutch Slow Food Foundation has compiled a list of 'endangered' regional products, including Gouda and Leiden farm cheese, Texel sheep cheese, Maastricht veal pie and Oosterschelde crab. To promote slow food products, regional Slow Food groups organise events to introduce members to the preparation and background of regional specialities. The generation that still knows these dishes 'from the old days' will certainly warmly recommend them.

Regional dishes

Small as the Netherlands may be, the country has several clearly identifiable regional cuisines. Groningen, for example, was one of the first provinces where spices were used liberally, not only in the region's famous cake but also in 'hot beer', brown ale that includes cinnamon and cloves.
By their own account, the Frisians are *swietbekken* – that is, they have a sweet tooth – as traditional treats such as sugar loaf and rice with raisins and

currants attest. Overijssel cuisine has seasonal specialities such as *balkenbrij* (a dish made with offal, buckwheat flour and raisins) in winter, summer prunes with smoked bacon, and *humkessoep*, a soup of potatoes, green beans and white beans in the autumn. Long ago, farm labourers in Utrecht got their energy from *vijfschaft*, a hearty meal of brown beans, carrots, potatoes and smoked sausage.

Bare bums

The provinces south of the major rivers – the Rhine, Maas and Lek – have strikingly different cultural traditions. 'Above the rivers', as the Dutch put it, people are fond of sturdy food; 'below the rivers', a more exuberant attitude prevails.
The southern provinces of Brabant and Limburg have rich culinary traditions, full of festive titbits. The traditional Brabant coffee table consists of various types of bread, sandwich toppings, soup, salads, a hot meal dish and alcohol, and is the second bread-based meal of the day, after breakfast. The Limburg variant is a cold buffet of specialities such as mushroom ragout and asparagus.
Dishes from these provinces have humorous names such as *blote billetjes in het gras* ('bare bums in the grass', white beans with broad beans) and *nonnevotten*, crisp fried pieces dough resembling the bows of Limburg nuns. But despite the sometimes incomprehensible names, a visit to Limburg especially is absolutely recommended for every culinary visitor. ∎

02 Old kitchen in the Stedelijk Museum in Zwolle. The oldest part dates from the 16th century. The tiles on the walls and the fireplace date from the 18th century. Most utensils date from the 19th century 04 Chef Jan Klerq of restaurant 't Diekhuus in Terwolde inhales the odour of the herbs in a kitchen garden

index

Bold numbers refer to a chapter on
the corresponding headword.